MARRATIDE

William Martin (1925-2010) was born in New Silksworth, Co. Durham. During the Second World War, he was a radio technician in the RAF, based near Jodhpur, where he was inspired by Eastern religious and philosophical traditions. After being demobbed he became a gas fitter and later served in the Audiology Department of Sunderland Royal Infirmary, retiring as Head of Department. He lived in Sunderland for over half a century, after settling there during the 1950s.

He was an active member of CND for many years, taking part in the ritual boarding of nuclear submarines in Holy Loch, Scotland in 1961. He became an artist and had work purchased and exhibited by Sunderland Art Gallery. However, oil paints and a young family were not an easy combination, and poetry became his medium from the mid 1960s onwards.

For some years he wrote without any recognition, but in 1973 he had a book of poetry published to commemorate the Wearmouth 1300 Festival (*Tidings of our Bairnsea*). This was later followed by *Cracknrigg* (1983) and *Hinny Beata* (1987) with Taxus, and *Marra Familia* (1993) and *Lammas Alanna* (2000) with Bloodaxe. His retrospective, *Marratide: Selected Poems*, edited by Peter Armstrong and Jake Morris-Campbell, was published by Bloodaxe in 2025.

WILLIAM MARTIN

MARRATIDE
SELECTED POEMS

EDITED BY PETER ARMSTRONG
& JAKE MORRIS-CAMPBELL

Poems copyright © Estate of William Martin 2025
Introductory essays © Peter Armstrong & Jake Morris-Campbell 2025

ISBN: 978 1 78037 746 9

First published in the UK in 2025 by
Bloodaxe Books Ltd,
Eastburn,
South Park,
Hexham,
Northumberland NE46 1BS

www.bloodaxebooks.com
For further information about Bloodaxe titles
please visit our website and join our mailing list
or write to the above address for a catalogue.

LEGAL NOTICE

All rights reserved. No part of this book may be used or
reproduced, stored in a retrieval system, or transmitted
in any form, or by any means, electronic, mechanical,
photocopying, recording or otherwise, without prior written
permission from Bloodaxe Books Ltd.

Requests to publish work from this book
must be sent to Bloodaxe Books Ltd.

William Martin asserted his right under
Section 77 of the Copyright, Designs and Patents Act 1988
to be identified as the author of the work included in this book.

Cover design: Neil Astley & Pamela Robertson-Pearce.

Printed in Great Britain by Bell & Bain Limited, 303 Burnfield Road,
Thornliebank Glasgow G46 7UQ, Scotland, on acid-free paper
sourced from mills with FSC chain of custody certification.

This book is dedicated to the memory of Gordon Brown, friend of the author. In their joint early retirements they walked together forging new paths and understandings.

AUDIO RECORDINGS 🔊

These recordings made by Katrina Porteous of William Martin reading his poems and singing can be heard via Bloodaxe's SoundCloud audio library by scanning the QR code below; or go to https://soundcloud.com/bloodaxe-books/sets/william-martin-marratide

Poems in *Marratide*

1. The White Christ
2. The Bald Ship
3. A19 Hymn
4. Kildan Fragments
5. Marratide
6. Image Ark
7. Anna Navis
8. I Johnbird
9. Six Island Sunset
10. Midwinter Song
11. His Bright Silver
12. Durham Beatitude

Other poems

13. Arl
14. Tidings of our Bairnsea
15. Saint's men (*Easthope*)
16. Briar and Rose (*Cracknrigg*)
17. Childermass Dene (*Cracknrigg*)

Traditional songs sung by William Martin

18. Sair fyel'd hinny
19. Have you seen owt of my bonny lad
20. Three Songs

In the case of sequences from which extracts have been made for this edition, the recording includes the whole uncut sequence.

CONTENTS

- 9 PETER ARMSTRONG: *William Martin: Gravity Lines*
- 19 JAKE MORRIS-CAMPBELL: *William Martin: Slipstreams*
- 27 *A note on the choice of poems*
- 28 *Acknowledgements*

FROM Cracknrigg (1983)

- 30 When May Be Out
- 30 *from* Hen Meneu * The Old Bush
- 34 Crist Gwyn * The White Christ 🔊
- 37 The Even Ships
- 39 The Round Dance
- 41 The Bald Ship 🔊
- 44 *from* A19 Hymn 🔊
- 47 *from* Kildan Fragments 🔊
- 50 Marratide 🔊

FROM Hinny Beata (1987)

- 54 *from* Malkuth
- 65 Wiramutha Helix
- 87 *from* Mothergate
- 89 *from* Anna Marra Missa
- 89 Moreneta
- 91 Song of the Cotia Lass
- 94 Song: 'We'll rise in the morning'

FROM Marra Familia (1993)

- 97 *from* Image Ark 🔊
- 106 Song: 'Will dayligone fash'
- 108 *from* Anna Navis 🔊
- 120 *from* Triptych
- 121 Slogan Bread

FROM **Lammas Alanna** (2000)

124   Aforeword
128   Mort Tiamat
130   Psalm
131   Quest
134   *from* I Johnbird 🔊
137   Maytime
139   Scordie
143   Exile
144   The Seafarer
148   Bede's Going
149   Six Island Sunset 🔊
153   Midwinter Song 🔊
157   *from* In Easthope
160   *from* Images from Samuel Palmer
163   Bairnseed
166   *from* Song: 'We meet at the lamp'
168   Song: 'As aa was gannin through Chester-le-Street'
170   *from* His Bright Silver 🔊
174   Song: A Wearside version 'It's O but aa ken well'
176   *from* Durham Beatitude 🔊

179   NOTES

PETER ARMSTRONG
William Martin: Gravity Lines

> I try for that oneness in my poems, but
> They also contain bits of promise, some
> Sorrow and a measure of resurrection.
> I am not hack led.
> To make new is art's speciality
> And man's only hope.
>
> from 'First a Word at the Beginning'
> in *Easthope* (Ceolfrith Press, 1970)

Early Life

William ('Bill' to his friends) Martin was born in 1925 in Silksworth, a pit village in the east of County Durham, long since swallowed into the outskirts of Sunderland. Apart from a period in World War II when he served in the RAF, he lived there and in other parts of Sunderland the whole of his life. He grew up in a milieu equally immersed in Methodism and the Mine. As he put it succinctly in his notes to his second pamphlet, *Tidings of Our Bairnsea*:

> 'My father and his father were miners
> their dust is in my spit'
>
> Carried behind banners
> Still there
>
> Great Grandfather Ralph
> A shipwright and independent preacher
> When told by police
> That he might be 'locked up'
> For preaching on Sunderland Town Hall steps
> Said he would 'sing and praise God'
> Till they were glad to let him out [1]

In a nutshell there you have the essence he distilled in his poetry: a profound social connection with the now disappeared industrial communities of the North-East, beneath and around which extend the spiritual grounds not only of his childhood Methodism, but of the deep Northumbrian history of Cuthbert, Hilda, Bede and Caedmon. Nor, for all his grounding in his own part of the world, was he in any trivial sense a "local" poet as his field of vision was enriched from the literatures and imageries of Wales, Ireland, India and ancient Babylonia.

His childhood was that of any boy growing up in his community, although his sharp recollection of it in adulthood and old age was unique. He played the street games that crop up repeatedly in his poems such as Mount-a-Kitty, a cross between leapfrog and a ruck, and Jack-Shine-the Magi, a night-time hide-and seek (see notes to the poems). He explored the woods and fields around his home village, delving into the wooded denes and playing perilously around the gravity wagonway that ran close by Silksworth. On this the trucks full of coal bound downhill for the staithes on the River Wear hauled the empty trucks back uphill via a rope-and-pulley system. In the absence of any engine noise, the children had to keep wary eyes and ears open for signs of approaching trains. He knew the emotional heft of Methodist hymnody, and was 'Carried behind banners' that were borne every year behind brass bands to the immense gathering that was and still is the Durham Miners' Gala.

He left school aged 14 in the summer of 1939, and over the next three years worked in various semi-skilled jobs: in the village cinema, a local foundry, as a groundsman at the miners' welfare sports ground, and as a gas maintenance fitter. With wartime, he joined the Air Training Corps (ATC) as well as the Home Guard, and served as an Air Raid Patrol volunteer, but it was the ATC that held his real interest; so it was that he volunteered for the RAF aged 17, receiving his papers on his 18th birthday in 1943.

War Service

Bill trained as a radio operator, being posted to several sites across England for training and service. Although his political thinking was still in its formative period at this time, we can see it developing between his boyhood willingness to swear allegiance to the Crown as a Boy Scout ('I don't know what I was thinking about') and his silent refusal on signing up ('when I came to join the RAF, I had to swear allegiance to the queen [sic]... And you all had to say it out loud; well, I never said it.' [2] During his early RAF service, he also found himself 'on jankers' for failing to salute his commanding officer.

In late 1944 he was posted overseas to India, sailing in an aged, slow troop-ship, enduring terrible sea-sickness across a very rough Atlantic and a not-much-better Mediterranean before becoming 'more human' crossing the Indian Ocean and landing in Bombay (Mumbai). From there he travelled to Jodhpur, a staging-post for air force and civilian aircraft crossing India. Very soon after arrival he became ill with typhoid and was hospitalised with a high fever. Drifting in and out of consciousness, his condition was complicated by malaria, and there was little hope of his recovery. Indeed, nursing staff thought him so near death and so far from awareness that they took to using his room for changing in and out of uniform. In later life he laughingly attributed his recovery not only to their nursing care, but to his dim awareness of feminine forms moving around him. His recovery was slow, at first in Jodhpur. Then, still ill enough to require transport via stretcher, he was flown by Douglas Dakota to Karachi, where he watched from the island of Manora as fishermen threw their nets into the sea. Then, via a series of transit camps ('Always transit camps') he eventually rejoined his service unit.

Three further key experiences occurred during his service in India that would inform and connect several strands in his writing and personality.

The first, shortly after his leaving hospital, was his unit's period of leave at the hill station at Mount Abu in Rajasthan, including a visit to the sacred Jain site on the mountain there. This not only 'stuck in my mind as a kind of sacred place', but connected to his sense of the medieval Europe of his imagination and later reading: of wandering holy men and sacred sites rich with intricate carvings, texts and figures. Important also was an encounter here with the sacred-as-feminine, a counter-weight to the orthodoxy of his upbringing. Undoubtedly an epiphany for the poet-to-be, it was long in maturing into the forms it took in into his later work.

Second came the atomic bombing of Hiroshima and Nagasaki. 'When the bombs were dropped…that night I prayed…and I realised that I was talking to myself; there was nobody there listening. That experience started a passage to atheism.' I recall a conversation with Bill in the 1980s when he made the unforgettable statement: *I'm an atheist – but only as far as God's concerned*. In other words, while he retained a lifelong affinity with the communal strength of his early religious socialisation, his sense of the sacred, which deepened over the years of his atheism, came radically adrift from its traditional Western formulations. Even his much later engagement with Anglo-Saxon and Celtic traditions of Christianity was based, not on any doctrines, but on the art and attitudes that connected his 'wandering holy men' of India to figures such as Cuthbert of Lindisfarne; the intricacies of a Jain temple to those of the great pages of the Gospel books of Lindisfarne, Kells and Bishopwearmouth/Jarrow where his own 'back yard' of Sunderland connected to a deeper history.

The third 'Indian experience' crystallised the values of colliery lodge and chapel into an explicit political stance. Following the end of hostilities, Bill's unit found themselves – while still serving with the RAF – operating in a semi-military, semi-civilian environment, servicing aircraft and waiting to be demobbed. Despite, or because of this more relaxed atmosphere, their commanding officer decided that they should embark on a regime of formal, full-dress colour-hoisting parades and kit inspections. In any environment, the absurdity of this for men simply going about their none-too-military work while awaiting discharge would have caused resentment. In the heat of India, after years of serving with little formal "kit", the idea was inflammatory: 'so the…unit met in darkness in the cookhouse and decided they weren't going to do [this]; they were going to work. It was later called a strike, but it wasn't a strike against work, it was against doing these silly things.' When the men followed through on this intention, the commander called in the armoured cars of the local Maharajah's army to face the 'strikers'. After a stand-off the C.O. backed down and more senior officers came in to settle the situation, but several factors in the experience can be seen as deepening Bill's attitudes: there was the willingness of the powerful to coerce and use unjustified violence against the less-powerful; the working-class capacity for collective action that carried through to his experience of the miners' strikes of the 70s and especially the 80s; and then the care of his comrades towards himself. Bill was the youngest member of the unit and the older men instructed him to remain in quarters rather than run the risks that they were prepared to face. Lastly, we know from Bill's papers that he was aware of the vengeful injustice that the authorities meted out to servicemen involved in this and other "mutinies" at this time, picked out because of their Communist sympathies, despite there being no evidence of a politically-driven conspiracy.[3] 'I called myself a Socialist from then on.'

After the War
Following this political awakening, he listened to political soapbox speakers on Sunderland bomb-sites, joined the Labour Party League of Youth, mixing with like-minded young people and meeting his wife-to-be Winsome (Win) Groves, the daughter of the one-time Labour mayor of West Hartlepool. But he was quite quickly disillusioned with the degree to which a Labour government would bring about Socialism as he understood it: 'I thought the possibilities of Socialism coming by the Labour Party were quite strong… But experiences taught me that it wouldn't be.' He also joined and was active in CND. His son Graham writes: 'He was an early CND supporter and joined the demonstration at Holy Loch when the nuclear submarines were symbolically stormed by demonstrators in canoes. He was a strong supporter

of the Committee of 100 which advocated filling the jails beyond capacity, but was restrained in that regard by Mam.'

Bill and Win married in 1950, setting off for their honeymoon on Win's battered BSA motorcycle, Bill the pillion passenger. Their first home was a small, former miners' cottage. Their first son, Graham, was born in 1953, and their second, Keith in 1957, when they moved into a new two-bedroomed council house. His first artistic efforts were in painting, from the early 1950s ('I think there'd been a crisis: me father'd died and me mother was dying, and maybe that influenced me'). He went to courses run by Durham County Council, painting in oils and drawing, exhibited with a Sunderland art club, working in what he called a very simple way but found by the mid 1960s that a two-bedroom house with growing children simply had too little space for him to carry on his art seriously. If his artistic gifts were thwarted at this stage, his imagination found exercise in his family life; constructing a pipework system running in and out the family's coal fire to better heat their sitting-room (it worked excessively); and his son Graham writes of an amusement he devised for the children: 'Dad also invented a way to modify a stirrup pump to connect to a gas tap in the wash house and to fill balloons with town gas, allowing us, as children, to send messages high into the sky, across the region and possibly further! A worldwide vision from a wash house had links with his poet vision of course! he also invented a way of creating a string fuse using saltpetre which led to spectacular, though safe, aerial explosions!' Quite how safe we can only wonder. What we can see here is the playfulness we also find in his poetry's continued references to his own childhood games. The family later bought a modest semi-detached house, Easthope, sitting under the limestone outcrops of Tunstall Hills (Maiden Paps is its older name, and as named in the poetry) where both Bill and Win lived for the rest of their lives.

His earlier graphic gifts found later expression in his cover designs for the poetry collections and his increasing weaving of visual material into his texts. He composed these from photographs, photocopies, medieval texts and images and examples of different letterings, meticulously cut and pasted into his typescripts.

After the war, Bill had returned to his work as a gas fitter. In 1953 he took up a post as audiology technician, working at the Sunderland Royal Infirmary until he retired to concentrate on his poetry, aged 57, in 1982. Over this period, his life fell into a series of steady rhythms, each of which fed into the content and structures of his poetry. In the years immediately following the war he made annual pilgrimage to the Miners' Gala at Durham, that Anne Stevenson described as 'the climactic point of the year'[4] for him. He was present in 1951 following the Easington Colliery Disaster. He continued to attend until the end of his life. From 1983, he and his close friend Gordon D. Brown devised a walking route from Easthope to St Cuthbert's shrine at Durham Cathedral, largely along the disused railway lines that had previously been his means of travelling to the Gala when he was 'carried on the shoulders' (see Jake Morris-Campbell's account of this walk). Each work-day he would walk down from his home at the edge of Sunderland to the infirmary, along the Thornhill road, past the premises of the Little Sisters of the Poor, both finding their place in the poems, especially 'Wiramutha Helix'. Climbing back up the hill again each evening, the Maiden Paps would frame his view. Friday evenings were often given over to readings at Morden Tower; Wednesdays to evening trips to Birtley and the famous folk club of the Elliotts, to listen and sing.

Given the apparent discrepancy between this 'quiet life' and the visionary tenor of his verse, it is understandable that Anne Stevenson should place Bill Martin in a category of poets whose private and professional lives remained distinct from the imagination of their poetry.[5] But I want to make the case for continuity between the life and the work. I want to stress the way these daily and yearly rhythms connected his Socialist vision to the practicalities of a working life in the NHS; the way that a continuous reaching after 'the suppressed feminine principle'[5] connected to his own hands-on life in a caring role and his wife Win's career as a school teacher; and, given the appeal his work makes to the ear, it's difficult not to see a connection between his work in audiology and the poetry. Bill Martin's life as a poet was not disjunct from his working life in the way Wallace Stevens's was; instead, he raised it into the song of his overall vision.

Martin the Poet

Bill's development as a poet began with attendances at poetry readings in Sunderland and at Newcastle's Morden Tower, which in 1964 became the fulcrum of the North-East poetry renaissance, centred around the figures of Basil Bunting and Tom Pickard. Although he was to develop a body of work quite distinct from anyone else's, Bill Martin shared with these figures, as with Barry MacSweeney, an approach that placed orality and aurality at the centre of a poem's being. 'Hearing poetry read was the beginning of it,' he tells his friend Gordon D. Brown in 1999.[7]

The earliest evidence we have of his own work are three quite distinct pieces showing the poet feeling for a form that could contain his vision and match his voice: the unpublished creation myth *Arl the Beginninger*, and two pamphlets, *Easthope* and *Tidings of Our Bairnsea*. While all three contain the elements of his mature work (as shown by his decision to reprint text from both *Easthope* and *Bairnsea* in his final collection) they also demonstrate features that Bill Martin was to move away from. *Arl* sees him creating a myth from scratch, whereas his later practice was to explore creative cross-fertilisations between the worlds of early Christianity, Indian and Mesopotamian mythologies and the collective experience of the mining communities from which he sprang. It also largely relies on a longer line and more 'solid' stanza forms than his later work. *Bairnsea* experiments with some concrete methods and the shortening of the line to a point where it appears on the page more vertically than laterally. And while the forms of the short poems in *Easthope* are sufficiently in keeping with the later work for their re-working and inclusion in his final work *Lammas Alanna*, they lack the overall shape he increasingly felt for in his later poetry. As he shares with Brown: 'All the books since then I've tried to make them not individual poems, but to have some connections through them.' Although these differences are very clear on the page, a *listener* would hear more commonalities than discrepancies between the early and the mature work; although he had not settled on satisfactory *form*, he was already operating with the tone, timbre, and musicality he was to refine throughout his writings.

He had published *Easthope* in 1970, and in 1973, as part of the celebrations marking the 1800th anniversary of the founding of St Peter's monastery on the north bank of the Wear, *Tidings of Our Bairnsea* appeared. He read his work both in Sunderland and at Morden Tower, but it would be another ten years before his first full-length collection was published. In the mid 1970s he met the poet Roger Garfitt, then writer-in-residence at Sunderland Poly-technic, who encouraged him to join the poetry workshop there, but Bill remained indifferent if not hostile to that culture as alien to his own path (he once scolded me for talking too much about it). But through Roger, he also came to know Frances Horovitz, and in 1980 Anne Stevenson and her then partner Michael Farley, who was in process of launching Taxus Press. It says something of the impact that meeting Bill – and reading and hearing his poetry – has on others that these four entirely different poets (not to mention the editors of this selection) were immediately attracted to the man and the work. The connection with Farley led to the publication of *Cracknrigg* in 1983 and *Hinny Beata* in 1987. There followed *Marra Familia* in 1993 from Bloodaxe, and his final collection *Lammas Alanna* in 2000.

Bill's readings were extraordinary. Unlike Bunting, who read in a self-conscious 'Northumbrian' that I don't believe any native of Northumberland or County Durham ever spoke, Bill read in an unexaggerated but heightened register of his own natural speaking voice. The effect was mesmerising. Although he did not read in public until 1970, by the mid-70s, when I first heard him, he was an accomplished reader, holding an audience effortlessly over the length of his extended sequences. As if his spoken poems were not song-like enough in themselves, he would intersperse spoken passages with singing, whether his own songs, snatches of hymnody or extracts from North-East folksong both serious and comical. The effect was something akin, one imagines, to attending shamanic incantations. And then, without obvious transition, once the reading concluded, he would be in conversation with a friend or other audience member, quite unaffected, modest, with a ready and characteristic laugh.

It was unfortunate that his reading and singing were affected by late-onset asthma as both the illness itself and the treatments (as many singers know to their costs) impair the reading and singing voice. His last days were also affected by growing memory-loss. We are indebted to yet another poet-friend and admirer Katrina Porteous for capturing Bill's reading voice in the selection that can be accessed in tandem with this book (see above).

Bill died in 2010, aged 85. He was survived by his wife Win, his sons and grandchildren; and, we might add, by his poems. We hope this new selection will bring them to the attention of a new readership.

1. From 'About the Author' in *Tidings of Our Bairnsea* (Wearmouth Festival 1973):

2. All quotations from conversations between Bill Martin and Gordon D. Brown are from recordings made by Gordon D. Brown in 1999.

3. For further reading see: a report in *The Observer*, 4 August 1986, and *Mutiny in the RAF– the Air Force Strikes of 1946* by David Duncan, The Socialist History Society, Occasional Papers Series: No 8 original printed version ISBN 0 9523810 6 0. Available at:
https://www.socialisthistorysociety.co.uk/?page_id=179

4. Anne Stevenson, *About Poems and how poems are not about* (Newcastle Centre for the Literary Arts/Bloodaxe Books, 2017). For remarks on William Martin's poetry see pp. 67-70.

5. Anne Stevenson, ibid.

6. Roger Garfitt, *The Guardian*, 17 October 2010. Available at:
https://www.theguardian.com/theguardian/2010/oct/17/william-martin-obituary

7. Gordon D. Brown, ibid.

JAKE MORRIS-CAMPBELL
William Martin: Slipstreams

Ten years ago, I sat nervously in Newcastle University in an introductory meeting for the PhD I'd just begun. I was talking about my sense of poetry from the North-East, wondering who else from here had written about this place. My supervisor, Bill Herbert, rose to his feet. Scanning his bookshelves, Bill withdrew a copy of William Martin's *Cracknrigg*. I didn't know it then, but it had only been five years since the death of Bill Martin. Whether he intended to set this in motion or not, one Bill had passed another Bill over. The wheel was in spin. Several months later, I was in the dining-room of Martin's son, Graham, books and photos scattered about the table and OS Explorer 308 spread out on the floor. I'd tried, using the poems as my guide, to recount the course of Bill's summer solstice pilgrimage from Sunderland to Durham. I'd used a highlighter to mark out what I thought was the route – and got it mostly right. But Graham thought there was a dog-leg missing, some turn not accurately plotted. 'You need to speak to Peter Armstrong,' he said.

So, in 2016, with Peter as our chief helmsman, we set off to beat the bounds of Bill's Northern Camino. I'd spent a year immersed in the poems, but now I wanted to walk them back into the landscape, to see how their cadences felt against the contours they described. Along with Peter and his wife Christine, I was joined by three other poets connected to Newcastle: Jason Lytollis, Kris Johnson and John Challis – the latter two of whom have recently published their debut collections with Bloodaxe. The poetry world is a small one, and while the inception story I'm telling here might, to the outsider, contain a nepotistic odour, the energy of Bill's poems and the subjects they broached ought to command a bigger orbit. As more and more people began coming along on our little jolly on the third Saturday in June, I realised that a bigger story was beginning to coalesce. In this, his centenary year, I want to make the case that the poems of William Martin deserve to be read and celebrated widely.

As I studied and thought about Bill's poems – spending many hours lost in bewildering references and learning about the figures and movements to whom he was alluding – I also began working on my own full-length collection. I'd put two pamphlets out into the world and was beginning to feel, through the writing that was merging around my PhD, that I had the early stages of a manuscript. Those readers, and I expect they will be legion, who have gone through the process of assembling a first collection will know what I mean when I say I fretted for years over how best to organise the poems and how they might speak to each other. Reading Bill's work became a massive aid in this process: as I travelled through his collections, I began to get a sense of how motifs might be best arranged, and how singular, short lyrics might riff off longer sequences.

To read Bill Martin's poetry is often to be plunged into the durational experience of the poem-sequence, but there are also breezier moments, such as 'Bede's Going', a wonderful 17-line encapsulation of the Northumbrian credo which so inspired his work. Where an intensity of vision is necessarily rendered across multiple pages, readers often feel their way into the language by degrees, testing out the vernacular of Bill's voice, grappling with his cultural touchstones, and absorbing the ebb and flow of his rhythms. To the serious reader of poetry, the sequences presented here offer a chance to be engaged in a process of sustained world-building. For those honing their craft, which we surely all always are, immersion in Bill's cosmos requires of us an attentive close reading which reaps the richest rewards.

Bill's power as an orator was frequently said to be incantatory, the performance of his poems bordering on shamanic ritual, an effect that comes through as much in a modern-day reading as it does in memoriam. In the *Guardian* obituary[1] written by his friend and fellow poet Roger Garfitt, Bill was positioned as a 'cantor for his community', his poems discussed as having the power to 'restore the collective symbols, releaf the ikons with gold'. The photograph used to celebrate Bill's life shows him in front of Bede's Memorial Cross at Roker. Seen on the cliff-top where, in 1904, the townspeople of Sunderland finally erected a monument to their most famous son, the Venerable Bede, who was known as the Father of English History, it's no surprise that Bill wanted to associate himself with Bede, the person who did more than any other in the Early Middle Ages to join the remote kingdom of Northumbria to continental religious currents and lineages of skilled craftsmanship – stained glass making and pandect production were imported to the Wearmouth-Jarrow monasteries of Bede's patch via the artisans of Gaul and Rome. Like Bede, Bill is a scholar and scribe whose canon must be considered as European as it is English.

There is another kernel. We see it in the two author photos on the back cover of this book – Bill proudly stood in front of the Silksworth Lodge banner at the Durham Miners' Gala. Dozens of these National Union of Mineworkers banners were – and still are – defiantly trooped into Durham on the second Saturday of July for what is known locally as The Big Meeting. Bill's pilgrimage may have had medieval foundations – the relics of Saint Cuthbert were made peripatetic, ferried around Northumbria in the 9th and 10th centuries to eventually settle at Durham – but the parades since the 19th century were firm working-class appropriations. Roger Garfitt saw how in Bill's poetry, just as in his life, these two elements weren't at odds, but rather hewn from the same bedrock: 'to Bill there was no division: the primitive Christianity of the monasteries had surfaced again in the close community of the pit villages and their long political struggle.' [2]

But we live after the end of the pits. As I'm writing this, the UK's last coal-fired power station at Ratcliffe-on-Soar has just finished operations. As a millennial Northerner born at the tab-end of the 1980s, why should I be interested in such sooty depictions? I think Bill's poetry offers a clue: more than simply a veneration of blood, sweat and toil, his poems address the deep-seated camaraderie of the Durham miners, asking us to contemplate what life might be missing without their kinship structures, while gesturing to universal questions of faith and belonging.

Each time I walk away from the garden of Easthope, Bill's former home in the foothills of the Maiden Paps (Tunstall Hills in the Sunderland suburbs), I ask myself what I'm doing. Each time I arrive in Durham six or seven hours later, I know the answer: to share in the simple joy of being with others. His grandchildren assembled to walk in his honour, but so too had a group of people who were essentially strangers. Storyteller Hugh Lupton reminds us that 'there is a tradition among the travellers that when you tell a story, the person you heard it from is standing behind you'.[3] It strikes me that Bill's poetry, drawing on the immediacy of the oral tradition, works in this way: we hear that chain of voices reaching back into the brine of the deep past. The Spanish have a term for this: *acompañar* – to accompany, walk with. As we walk to Durham Cathedral now each summer with Bill as our spirit guide, his poems not only chaperone us, enriching the landscape features through which we might otherwise obliviously pass, they propel us forward, acting as way markers for the type of future we might want to make manifest.

It's funny the way poetry makes connections. In early 2019 I was approached by Shut Out The Light Films, a Liverpool-based production company who were working on a feature-length film about the Durham Miners' Gala. Director Daniel Draper travelled up to Sunderland to meet me and Graham Martin. We took Daniel to the trig point at the top of Tunstall Hills and showed him William Martin country. Looking out from here, it's not difficult to see how the geography of Houghton and Seaham, Fulwell and Hylton inspired poems like his 'Wiramutha Helix'. With Sunderland and its vistas foregrounded, Tyneside and Northumberland's Cheviot off further to the north, and the headland at Hartlepool and Cleveland Hills marking the southern boundary of his outlook, the sense of Bill's world spooling out from this origin-point is clear.

Speaking about this view in 1990, Bill said: 'I only have to go to the top of them [Tunstall Hills] to see the land of my fathers.'[4] It's a vista, I told Dan, that Bill felt safe and comfortable in, but certainly not one which restrained his imaginative roaming. Back in the living-room at Easthope, we spoke about the dialogue Bill seemed to open between a mining community in North-East England and icons from around the world. It's a vision which had the Welsh White Goddess Cariadwen naturally alongside Tiamat, the Great Goddess of Babylonian myth, and the words to kids' street games ('Eeny-meeny-macker-racker') circling a reproduction of the Black Madonna of Montserrat. Bill was a Do It Yourself artist making zines out of literal cut and paste mixed media methods before it was fashionable to do so. In 'Durham Beatitude', which remembers the Easington Colliery Disaster of 1951, he asks 'what kingdom without common feasting?' It's a message that chimed with Dan and, three years later, when he returned to the North-East to film proceedings on Big Meeting Day, revellers at the Racecourse in Durham were treat to a cinematic interpretation of Bill's poem. I urge you to watch the short clip,[5] which combines recent and archival footage of the Gala with the author's bardic recitation of the poem.

Other connections followed. In 2016, I took Bill's rhetorical question from 'Durham Beatitude' and began asking it at conferences and symposia and within different publications. The Dark Mountain project were early supporters, publishing my essay on Bill in the 2016 edition of their journal, *Uncivilised Poetics*,[6] as were *Wild Court*,[7] the international poetry journal based out of King's College London. I then did what all Early Career Researchers are supposed to do and contacted the organisers who would give me a platform to talk about a subject that others might deem esoteric. In 2018, I enthused widely about Bill's work: at The Poetics of Faith conference at the University of York; at the Orientations conference at the University of Nottingham; and, closer to home, I was delighted to speak about Bill's pilgrimage at the 'Living Otherwise' workshop at the Thought Foundation in Birtley. At all of these events, I began to get a sense that Bill's concept of 'Marradharma' – the sacred unity of his social, spiritual and political beliefs – was cutting through. In an increasingly partisan country growing sceptical of its leaders while disdaining its legacy media, and in a cultural epoch increasingly riven by polarisation and seemingly facing one existential threat after another, something about the principled integrity of Bill's neologism was starting to make waves.

Media attention on Martin following his death also recently piqued the curiosity of the BBC. In April 2022, I broadcast an essay on Radio 3. 'Walking with the Ghosts of the Durham Coalfield'[8] was my way of marking Bill's pilgrimage and adding further interpretation to his poems. In a monologue featuring my memories of first walking Bill's route in 2016, I recounted how, early in the day, I was asked by Graham whether I would carry his father's ashes to the cathedral. 'Asked' was, in retrospect, probably too polite a description. When I turned up, Graham had already prepared the vessel – a ram's horn which his dad had once picked up in a field outside the city. I duly carried the keratin urn, which had been hastily sealed with gaffer tape, and at select points along the way we scattered some of Bill's ashes to the wind, reading stanzas from 'Malkuth' as we did so. Of course, this wasn't the first time Bill had graced the airwaves. In 1982, he read on the BBC's *Poetry Now* programme.

I mention these efforts not to ingratiate myself, but to note the growing appetite, both from independent producers and established outlets, to listen to poetry that at one time was considered parochial. Indeed, as Patrick Kavanagh reminds us:

> Parochialism and provincialism are direct opposites. The provincial has no mind of his own; he does not trust what his eyes see until he has heard what the metropolis – towards which his eyes are turned – has to say on the subject. This runs through all activities. The parochial mentality on the other hand is never in any doubt about the social and artistic validity of his parish. All great civilisations are based on parochialism – Greek, Israelite, English […] To be parochial a man needs the right kind of sensitive courage and the right kind of sensitive humility.[9]

This, then, is the nature of the parish Martin's work describes: the locally rooted mindset from which his work takes imaginative flight out into the global community. It is the community of Silksworth, where the artificial ski slope has been laid over the pit mound. It's the wider county of Durham, its 'Spoke into hub-city waiting' ('Anna Navis'), and it is the international fraternity to whom his lines from 'Abuba Bide' so gestures: 'It is a way of arms linking / A dance of life'. Here at the beginning of 2025, it is finding new form in the City of Sunderland, a place undergoing a cultural renaissance and reinstating its commitment to the arts via its Music City initiative and the ambitious Crown Works Film Studios being built at the former Pallion Shipyard on the banks of the River Wear. But it's also the community of poets whose work and traditions preceded and surrounded Bill, inspiring his craft: William Blake, George Mackay Brown, David Jones, Anne Stevenson, Kathleen Raine, Gillian Allnutt. A slapdash literary genealogy that may seem, but it gives a sense of Martin's bent and the writers he might be judged beside. Ultimately, I think, he was a Mackem – they of Sunderland who built the ships and were the 'makers' of the industrial age. That egalitarian spirit with its graft and grit lives on in Bill's verse. From the Wear to the World might sound like a clunky campaign slogan, but it encapsulates, I think, the mission at the heart of this book – to bring a forgotten voice from these shores back into a wider public consciousness.

But the wider culture is a tough one, and we'd do well not to sugarcoat the challenges. I don't intend to use this platform to launch into polemic, but the ecology into which this book is launched is far from auspicious. It's a culture in which more than a third of adults have given up reading for pleasure[10] and in which children's reading enjoyment has fallen to its lowest level in nearly two decades.[11] A challenging climate, certainly, and that's without mentioning the myriad other divisions – so well documented and lamented, to the point of their ubiquity numbing us. But I think Bill's work is ultimately uplifting and offers us, dare I say it, hope.

When, at the 150th anniversary of the Durham Miners' Gala in 2021, Wallsend's *Emmerdale* star Charlie Hardwick gave a rousing delivery of 'Durham Beatitude' from a lectern in the cathedral so beloved of Bill and his Haliwerfolc, I knew that his legacy was in safe hands. For those yet to discover it, *Marratide* presents the curious reader with the perfect opportunity to find out why William Martin should be considered not just a custodian for the North-East, but an ambassador for poetry and its rich and interlocking seams of emotion, sound and intellect. For poets like Peter and I, working in his slipstream, he will always remain a figure of tremendous inspiration. If you've not yet had the pleasure of the William Martin experience, I am slightly envious, and half wish I could be back in that office a decade ago about to get to know him all over again.

1. https://www.theguardian.com/theguardian/2010/oct/17/william-martin-obituary.
2. Roger Garfitt, 'Walking Off the Fear', *Selected Poems* (Manchester: Carcanet, 2000), p.73.
3. Hugh Lupton, 'A Chain of Voices' in *The Dreaming of Place* (Norwich: Propolis, 2022).
4. William Martin in *The Page*, a supplement produced jointly by *The Northern Echo*, Northern Arts and Durham County Libraries. 10 July 1990.
5. https://www.youtube.com/watch?v=ML6aBdLdYjg.
6. Jake Morris-Campbell, 'What Kingdom Without Common Feasting?' Dark Mountain, Issue 10, *Uncivilised Poetics*, Autumn 2016.
7. Jake Morris-Campbell, 'Marratide: William Martin's Chorography of County Durham'. *Wild Court*, 3 June 2019. https://wildcourt.co.uk/2386/ – Accessed 10th November 2024.
8. https://www.bbc.co.uk/programmes/m0016jps – first broadcast 25 April 2022.
9. Patrick Kavanagh in *A Poet's Country*, ed. Antoinette Quinn (Dublin: Lilliput Press, 2003).
10. https://www.theguardian.com/books/article/2024/jul/24/more-than-a-third-of-uk-adults-have-given-up-reading-for-pleasure-study-finds – accessed 7th November 2024.
11. https://www.theguardian.com/books/2024/nov/05/report-fall-in-children-reading-for-pleasure-national-literacy-trust – accessed 7 November 2024.

A note on the choice of poems

William Martin published two early pamphlets, *Easthope* and *Tidings of Our Bairnsea*, and four full collections, *Cracknrigg*, *Hinny Beata*, *Marra Familia* and *Lammas Alanna*. Around the time of producing the pamphlets, he also wrote a long poem *Arl*, which he never published. A poster was also produced based on work he did in Gateshead schools on old street games he had played as a child. He refashioned earlier poems from *Easthope* and a passage from *Tidings of Our Bairnsea* for inclusion in *Lammas Alanna*.

Where a poem or section of a poem has been re-placed in this way, we have taken the latter version to indicate Martin's own preference and placed it accordingly. The exception is 'Song of the Cotia Lass', which he included in *Lammas Alanna*, but unaltered from its inclusion in *Hinny Beata* apart from the numbering of its sections. This has been included with the selection from that earlier collection.

While his style of writing was spare, his sequences were long. Therefore, difficult decisions faced us, not only as regards which poems to include and which not, but also about 'trimming' longer sequences in order to include a representative range of the work. Where this has been done, the aim has been to retain their overall architectural integrity. The full versions of all poems in *Marra Familia* and *Lammas Alanna* remain available from Bloodaxe Books.

With no small reluctance we decided against inclusion of material from both *Arl* and *Tidings of Our Bairnsea*, as including the whole of both poems would have been at the cost of later, more mature work. At the same time, we were unable to select from the poems without badly compromising their integrity. Hopefully they will see print at a later date.

ACKNOWLEDGEMENTS

This selection is drawn from William Martin's four full-length collections: *Cracknrigg* (1983) and *Hinny Beata* (1987) from Taxus Press; and *Marra Familia* (1993) and *Lammas Alanna* (2000), both still available from Bloodaxe Books. Poems from his first pamphlet *Easthope* have been taken from his own selection made for inclusion in *Lammas Alanna*.

Martin rarely submitted work to poetry magazines. Of the poems in this selection, 'Crist Gwin – The White Christ' and 'The Round Dance' appeared in *Passing Through*, ed. Roger Garfitt (Sunderland Polytechnic, 1979), while 'Marratide' and 'Durham Beatitude' first appeared in *Poetry Review*, Vol. 70, No 4 (1981), again, under Garfitt's editorship. Roger was early to recognise the significance of Martin's work and to put it on a national stage, maintaining that appreciation to the end of Martin's life in composing his *Guardian* obituary (17 October 2010).

Anne Stevenson quotations are taken from *About Poems and how poems are not about* (Newcastle Centre for the Literary Arts / Bloodaxe Books, 2017). Like Roger Garfitt, she was a passionate advocate for Martin's work.

Jake Morris-Campbell's introduction draws extensively on his paper 'Marratide: William Martin's Chorography of County Durham', *Wild Court* (King's College London, 2019).

Martin's conversations with Gordon D. Brown are taken from the digital archive of Graham Martin. The recordings of his readings (listed opposite Contents) were made by Katrina Porteous.

This selection of William Martin's poems would not have been possible without the encouragement and support of his son and literary executor Graham Martin. His was the original idea to mark the centenary of his father's birth with a new presentation of his poems, particularly bringing to a new readership work no longer available in print. He has given the editors invaluable access to his digital archive and has always made himself available to answer questions on his father's life and work.

FROM

Cracknrigg

(1983)

WHEN MAY BE OUT

Tid Mid Miseray
Carlin Palm
Paste-Egg Day

⋆   ⋆   ⋆

from HEN MENEU ⋆ THE OLD BUSH

1.

Dust days in genizah
Stored codex and scroll
Gold-leaf Eden bird
Initial inhabitation
Fiery sentinel angel
Stark nemeton dance
Fishy mother of darkness
Barbed umbilical path

3.

Do not speak to the wound
We are withered to him

Do not vintage the blood
She is whenceforth

Do not cry Eloi
Who is timbered alone?

Do not crack the glass darkly
Eat the bruised kingfisher
Sell the harvest now
Unmiracle the bread

5.

Hen meneu foments dawn
Maiden Paps on fire

Twice under dog-rose seen
Twice under elder-flower
Twice under bracken palms
Waving Jerusalem ride
Wren-alarm thicket-hide decoy-lark
Twice the haught-rib given her green

6.

Mysterium children
Flushed in the bushes
Beat dove
Startle wren
Wind cord-golden roots

One for the holdfast stem
Two for the flood
Three for the rosy babes
Shrived by her blood

Deluge of cock
Deluge of hen
Deluge of ladybirds
Fly away 'yem

Gone is the hearth
Gone is the fire
Gone are the children

7.

Under banner hoist
Under Jack shine
Under maggi light

Under lamp marsh
Under shift moon
Under cockerooso soon

Under broken crown
Under tumble hill
Under Johnnie
Under Jill

Under cockerel and hen
Under ten thousand men

Under everlasting feast
Under jasper and gold

Egger queen egger
All gone from the streets

8.

Children straggle Kinley Hill bridle
Barbed elect under hill

Harrow gripes dust sign
Holocaust hedges cleared

Memories roll stained eggs
Beacon to sore dene side

Scorched lark leads remnant
In burning bush wind

CRIST GWYN * THE WHITE CHRIST

1.

Cyntefin
Garland queen
Naked summer
Glossy green

Cyntefin
Thorn-bare
With blood-berries
Crows roosting

Cyntefin
Maytime
Rust there
I am dying

Cyntefin
Like cheese and bread
Walker taste
Your fresh buds

2.

Eyes stare through
Barbed-wire lashes
Unblinking
As birds flutter

Seven hedges
Seven robins
A blood-trail
To guide you

Flags litter branches
I am laid before furrows
Crow at each corner
Overgrown catafalque

3.

Morning star chorus
Comet of exile
Buttercup pentecost
White valley head

Wind-blown fields
Flakes of his snowing
Drifting against me
Smooth-tongued wonder

The brilliant frost
Words of death
The moment you said it
The finger

Black ice the same
Reflections of black
Howling and empty
Space between stars

Morning star chorus
Torrent of longing
Cosmic meltwater
Ingrown finger

4.

Albino blackbird
My singer
In Christmas greyness
Your wings flash

In woodland
The pretender lurks
You not frost
Sing of me

He is hiding
Rigid white shadow
But you are my whiteness
My fleeting oddity

Wagtail across path
You nip the frost
Kingdom's worm
Wriggling

He is silent
Jack of the wood
You have kingdom
In the throat

THE EVEN SHIPS

1.

Sickle cuts breaker
White horses shy from sea
Now will I arise

For sea-coal rakers
For Wednesday singers
For Thorn Hill nuns
For Jock-o-the-pit
For all the berries of autumn

2.

Three come sailing in
The knot-hole fipple carols

Wave-rut even ships bring
X.P.I. as spears hail

These west-blown thorns
Habitually reach to him

Bare but for prickle
Twisted in longing

Awaiting east blossom
And Yuletide fire promise

3.

When may be out
Cast of with ship
Some day in the morning
This road ends

Some day for sure
On Vinegar hill
With side split open
With thirsty cry

On Hollycarrside
On Thorn Hill banks
Our blinded children
Dance the last dance

What shall we play on Vinegar Hill?
Hitchydabber says Hollycarrside
Let's hoist the banner
Let's mountykitty
Let's skip let's tig
Let's dress the bride

* * *

THE ROUND DANCE

After IV Ezra 5.42 'He said to me: I will make my judgement like a round dance: the last therein shall not be behind, nor the first in front.'

1.

Reckity blue and a crowd of starlings
Hustle night over hill

Gulls follow
Umbrage-footed Jacob wrestles

Windy peewits watch
Starlings excited stop rolling night back

Angel in water-meadow mud
Trampled dandelion sun

2.

Rusty-winch hauling
White coble rides swell

He asked for a fish
Will beach-lore offer a stone?

Tears amid smoke
Stubble burning

White horses trample
The offshore parable

3.

Black-tongued crows
Smoke-signal carrion

Thorn-tree birds
Hear green buds stir

A child is named
Cheese and bread offered

Six bearers are ready
To wreathe his red berries

4. *(for Samuel Palmer)*

Root spread tree-bole beck-pool trickle
Dipper under overhang

Woodland skirt
Nest huge with eggs

Chestnut bough
All helping hands

Woodchatter seated piper
Hillrock figure

THE BALD SHIP

Sair fyel'd hinny
Sair fyrl'd noo
Sair fyel'd hinny
Sin 'aw kenned thou

1.

I sail the bald ship
In fog days Cariadwen

In milkygate coble
In frost days I winch

Crabs edge over pavement
Nightfall strides neap now

I cry callerherrin
I haul away fish

2.

It is night
Without comfort
Toil and horn going

No warm belly
Under sheet

I whisper to ice
I whisper to nothing
I touch a cold star
Cariadwen all grief

3.

Songs all night
At my door Cariadwen

I was Mabyn
Grown older

A green boy
To your dear
Ancient web

With may for your hair
And cowslips to kiss

And a hand-down suit
Which always fits

4.

Remember me when
Your new boy comes

Out of Bethlehem
Or Kyo or Esh

With his magi gifts
And his star on a stick

Will you wash him all over
With Magdala soap
And dry him with ringlets
Old whore till he pricks?

5.

It was the trick of love

Hand-reared for kingship
For you Cariadwen
Till all the songs ended
Bride song and groom song
Shrine-candle guttering
Spouse in my bed

6.

I walked the drilled
Fields with you
Parable lady

I came to your harvest
Bald like the sun

Flaming pate
Rowan hair
Ash blood on
Mountain banks

Bald and beautiful
They say I am

from **A19 HYMN**

Down in yon forest
There stands a hall
The bells of Paradise
I heard them ring

1.

Gannet splash

A drowning

Ship marks
Squabbling gulls

Furrow-eyed ploughman
Tumbleweed words…

Leaping ditches
Who goes there after them

Past sentinel winding heads
Along mourning beaches
Over black shingle…

Distant hills hail steeple rooster
Wind in his tail

No resting place for lost words
Driven across fields

To cliffs and bird-emptied shells
Their secret out

3.

Blood is west
Of his green day

Gibbet and tar
His trundling cart

White rooks coming
Across field stubble

Crimson-berry sunset
A flaming tree

White birds flock to it
Silently roosting

Corpus inscription
Iron frames his heart

5.

Three times denied
The morning cock

Three times
To thistle

Three times
To cuckoo spit

Once for seashore
Sun up out of it

Twice for fish
Baked at the rising

Three times for egg
Stained polished and rolling.

6.

Worn hill grass
Friday's worn hill grass
I'll sing you four
For worn hill grass

Four for kestrel
Flesh-eyed the first word

Four for pandect-calf
Flying from pasture

Four for winged cat
Fierce fledgling bringer

Four for bright angel-man
Gathering in

from KILDAN FRAGMENTS

*To commemorate the 50th anniversary
of the evacuation of the island community
of St Kilda on 29th August 1930*

1.

I will not fall
Though my frame be on fire

The same sun
Strikes Mary McQueen

She sits with her father and brother
Blazing feet on young gannets

For her and her only
Will I risk the Mistress Stone

We will swear together my Mary and I
Crucifix and people will witness

2.

Like most my first choice is fulmar flesh
But mackerel shoals are passing

I sit with my kin for the Mod
As every morning except Sunday in the Street

Mod or St Kilda Parliament
It makes no odds

Fish or fowl we have to decide
Last week we re-allocated the strips

5.

Sleep a night on Conachair
Awake a poet encompassed

Make music with wind and sea birds
Our song remnant is decried

Only Euphemia McCrimmon
Cares to remember

Her old-age stick
Thrust into sand

Rapt stones recall the
Dance of the fumar-share-out

6.

When sun divides glen
I should fear no evil

But who will walk for us
The long afternoon shadow

From death-house to grave circle?
If need be crossing the strips

Who tramples the last crop?

Mary Gillies went over in June
This August day St Kilda dies

We have killed the dogs
Yesterday Dunara shipped our beasts

Exodus remnant waits to board Harebell
Leaving bibles and corn

MARRATIDE

As aw was gannin t' Durham
Aw met wi' three jolly brisk women
Aw asked – what news at Durham?
They said – joyful days are cumin

1.

Constellations ride the shift over
Frost sticks to heel-plate click

Baccy is recovered
And rubbed before fire

Backscrubbed blue scars
Mark lean memories
Under the Hunter

Long rows rib hillside
Belts tighten under hunger

2.

Police-narks spy on gamblers' rock

Slagheap
The bones of fathers
Smokes across clover and buttercup

Larks
High as coin toss
Call warning

4.

Slow march
Pit closed
Drum beating death

Church waits
The Lord's my
To Crimmond
Small bell tolling

They bury him like a king

Now quick gay music going home
Clay mound left behind

5.

Crake-men cry special meeting
Bannerbearers
Elected leaders

From Chopwell to Easington
Harton to Evenwood
Lodges levy for widows
Lay plans for route
March in or march
Train or bus march

The field measures twenty by twenty
Black glinting harvest under seasons
Men and grass
Roots reaching fire
Crushed sun

Crushed fathers crape banners here
Cuthbert gazes
The living
With the dead
March to his Dunholm for rights
Meeting
Class wrestle
Brass and banners and pint froth
Flood gorge streets

In Framwellgate and Elvet
Sons dance to the drums' thump

6.

The haugh grows emblem edged

Silk samaritan
Suffer the children
Ownership Unity Lenin and Hardie
Cook Horner Hepburn Nye

I is not here…

After speechmakers
Drum signals return

Village children
Pass the news of bannerback

Band at each bar
Standard heroes

FROM

Hinny Beata

(1987)

from MALKUTH

Kingdom Lodge banner unfurled

> Man, Jack, it was a clivvor seet,
> Wi' scores of candles lit,
> As it was hauled inti dayleet,
> The last corve frat hi pit;
> Wi used ti hev a week or two
> Then when this 'eer wis up
> And mony a time byeth me and thoo
> Hes helped ti buss thi tyup
>
> from *The Bussen ov thi Tyup*
> by Matthew Tate, pub. 1898

1.

Eden's last shift and
The Tup is decked out

Her womb closes
On Genesis pages

Goaf contractions
Snuff out the light

But light is on the horns

They send away the Tup
From the shaft foot

The final corve
Caged to bank

The last coal
Out of her

2.

Tup was in Mothergate thrashing

Horns and hooves
Flashing by taper
And Davey

She speaks in the putter's curse

Little chance driver off the way

He sings with them all at the bussing

5.

Ground moves
under our feet

the goaf-roof collapses

spiralling steel rope rusts

pulley-wheel life
and death focus
razed and grassed

ground moves
under our feet

6.

Heaving eskhatos barley sea
Long eskhatos fetch

Last green
Waves break
On embankment

Blood in the waves
Blood in the waggons
Blood in the staithes' drop
Poppy-blood over the bar

7.

We are cast
Onto the ground
It was yesterday
In the morning

We are dead
In the ground
It was yesterday
In the morning

We roll away the
Good ground stone
It was yesterday
In the morning

We are whiskered
And yellow-brown
It was yesterday
In the morning

11.

She suckles him
Into plain words

If I cry cockerooso
Generations hop across

If I wait for
The banner
Coming hom
All rejoice

If I cross the
Golden river
It is the colour
Of going

If I rise with sheep
And kye from my bed
It is bonny at morn

13.

The path is
Indeterminate
At first

1822 line grown over

Track to the city cut across

Bridges down and
Crossings uprooted

Ghostly primal waggons
Through clouds of
Brick and tarmac

16.

Cuthbert's brief dream
And high resting place
Here before Durham

Winding-engine
And chimney-stack

Smoke shadow on ponds

Strings of spawn-waggons
Hauled and gravity-tallyed to top

17.

Show us the way
To Durham
Lasses with your
Dun-cow and milk

Show us the way
I can see the tower now
In my hindsight clear day

Show us the way
To his touching
Real foot of the
Shoreline with birds

Blackback and dunlin

Show us the way
To his kirk white in thorn
To his lost Haliwerfolc

18.

Over the top
Past a stretch
Of blue butterflies

Striking miners
Riddling for coal
Digging into embankment

A skin tickle like
Their forbear's
Early scratchings
The track hits a
Field of barley

20.

Walking away with
The seashore behind

Its seed-hiss reminds
Of the first shore

Askr and Embla there
Rooted and touching

Alpha-light catching each branch

What is light
Without object

Straight gate emission

Creation's first reflection

23.

Out of dust
And Genesis sand
She breathed him

Walking down to Hetton
On the longest day

But not the first collection

Lambton Hetton and Joicey
Have been here
By the trainful
Summers before
With fossil man

26.

Under Pytta's hill they walk

Rape-gold wide fields
Foil psalter-like the scarp

Hetton to Elvet
Picking them up

Kisses in steam and soot

Marriage flowers
In the psalter

28.

We knock at the emptiness

Bronze ring hand-lavished

The nave a cleared out
Space without banners

Word-bones without flesh

The screen a museum-piece fragment
Its resurrection dimly lit

33.

At seven in the morning
Motley band and bandsmen

At seven in the morning
Da's neck and legs

At seven in the morning
Flapping silk answer before them

At seven in the morning
Blowin in the wind my friend

35.

Black Madonna trees
They take yesterday
In the forest

In Mothergate
The body of her hauled
And hung with tokens

Nystagmus
Pulley-wheel eyes
Lamp the dark

Hidden of the foot
That passeth by

37.

It is black under
Waggon-way grass
And sleepers
Ripped out now

Black from in-bye
And all around the bank

Black like the song
Coming doon the waggon-way

Black with a pocket full of money

Black with a poke full of hay

40.

Away from the foot
That passeth by

Away from where men sojourn

They gather a
Natural harvest

Truth a share
Shift by shift

44.

The silk feast is a
Table set before us

Enemies all around

Band-led serpent coming down

A rag and bob-tail army

Slogans melting in
Sunlight at twelve

45.

Daydreams by Elvet station
Mothergate ending

Bridges down and
Hinterland lines
Ploughed over

Ryhope Murton and Hetton
Drawn in years ago
By the train-full

46.

Ghost-voices of Kropotkin
Cook and Keir Hardie
Echo from prison
E-Wing wall

I give you the end
As the song weakens

Only wind it in

Frail thread sounds
Twist to a ball

47.

Worm river-bend
Cradles them

Worm river-haugh rocks
Them laughing to sleep

Worm river-water dreams
For them over again

Worm river-mist
Covers their silk

WIRAMUTHA HELIX

Tell the bairns in their wilderness

  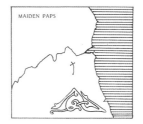

  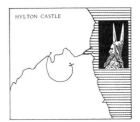

  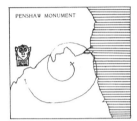
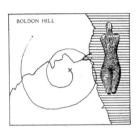 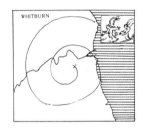 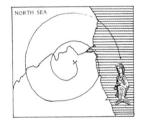

Rosy apple lemon and pear
A bunch of roses she shall wear
Gold and silver by her side
She shall be a bride

Take her by the lily-white hand
Lead her across the water
Kiss her eyes and lips on the hill so high
She is yesterday's daughter

Thorn Hill

1.

Thorn Hill is grown under
Concrete and tar

How many tongue-ties
Will lick the honey

Thorn Hill has a crack
Full of green fossil stars

How many blinded
Will see them rise

2.

I said to the wind
Blowing crow-smoke about her

How many nest-fires
Will Spring take to come

I said to the solstice-sun
Rolling low into dark

How many yellow beaks
How many tongues

3.

Thorn Hill is set groaning
By a silver-touch finger

How many blossoms
Will pollen her quick

Thorn Hill is a black bark
Split open tomorrow-tide

How many sick mornings
Will Eskhatos bring

Maiden Paps

4.

Corn over breast blown
Summer into harvest

Jostling ears confused…
Hiss of seed coming…

Path with crows
And golden hatchings

Helix unravels harvest
Crows scare the corn

5.

Voices come at last out of the spiral path
Out of twin hills

Cleft alined with
Pensher and Hastings

Due west through Fatfield and the Worm
And Cotia underground

The Tup decked out
Candle bristles singe

6.

Sea-root breasts are fossil
Reef dried out to desert

Ice gouging Hope House
Haunted by psyche clay

Well in forbidden wood
Plop pebbles 'a dare yu'

Who dashes in green light
Who holds a bairn's tongue

Silksworth Colliery

7.

(There will be a special meeting)
We all stand still

(In the Miners' Hall)
I touch your eyes to tears

(At seven o'clock)
I count to fifty while you hide them

I see day turning away from us
The moon is a dark faced Crake Man

8.

I am his shakey-down child
Silk banner up to chin

I hold his blue-scarred hand
Deep in cloth cap grass

I am raised to meet dawn
Slow on a green shoulder

I am in the whole field moving
As marra-wind ruffles

9.

Drum thumps its common pulse
I felt it all day

Ears and throat connect brass valves
I clip music to my feet

I dance the banner clef
Tassel notes Lodge at the heart of it

I will sing inarticulate words
Next year in Durham again

Hastings Hill

10.

Path through corn hedgeless
Lone fox under cover

His red tail trailing
To a bronze cist empty

Child bones glassed
Pressed noses steaming

Flesh fades away ageing
To metal classified

11.

Virgin from the hill
Crooks her arm under

Virgin on the steps
Guards reconstructed cist

Bone cracks like wood
Painted skin sunk in

She holds the bronze child
Plucked from green corn golding

12.

Sunrise March and September
From sea in cleft old breasts alined

Thread drawn out of Thorn Hill
Her bow tied to ravel-hill top

Lovers go on a bit
Pulling it slack again

White triangulation shadow
Leaping over paths

Hylton Castle

13.

Harm is out of the way
Lonely tower without light

Silent herald Tupp
(Horned Kronos Moses)

Unable to read the stone
Shielded from eyes

Shielded from her moon
Suddenly on castellation

14.

Fly again with puritan crows
Over battlefield housing estate

Spin pitch and toss down Pennywell banks
To 'waes me' castle to singing 'caad lad' ghost

'No acorn has fallen from this tree
To grow the wood to make the cradle

To rock the bairn into a man
Who'll lay me'

15.

We touch his apparition
He is a changeling

We lay a table before him
He plots against order

We feed him with greenery
He falls into autumn

We impale him on icicles
He spikes the harvest

Fulwell Mill

16.

White foul-well mill…
Empty handed sails…

White bleached limestone
Beacon on bright days

Lost canvas tacking
Her ghostly brig ballast

Dumped flint and sand
I saw three ships trimmed in black

17.

White mill her days are ground
To black bread staff

Broken fossil seed
Carbon-copy life

Wind through tarred fingers
Empty cross-arm hands

White mill I saw three ships
Crest-fallen over bar

18.

White mill your fixed arms
Are winded and seen through

Unfeathered unturned
Vibrating not pushed aside

Stone is fragmented
(All the King's horses

And all the King's menders)
Cemented into wall

Wearmouth

19.

Saints come out of age
Under ballast hills dumped

They walk east through shingle
Twined serpents at hand

They walk east out of grassed sand
Go east into shifting sand washed

Saints come out of age
They walk east on our pages

20.

He came to be venerable with them
Common words raised by common vision

Morning Star a coble from blackness
Fishers of men told where to cast

Spuggie-sparrow flying to a
Beginning of every wonder

Migrating wings take him
Now should we praise

21.

He aches out a history
His cold desert song

Leningrad feeling the nip
This hermitage speaking up

White vapour puffing
Inked words in and out

North arm and south arm
Await the star rising

Salterfen

22.

Are you coming out of Thorn Hill
Are you coming out of rock

Are you coming out of acorn
Tell the ships

Are you coming hissing white
Are you coming morning tide

Are you coming out of shell twist
Tell the ships

23.

I come without helm
To the rising

I come without wind
Salterfen

I come without words
To trap me all over

I come golden bowl
To share now and then

24.

Take the bowl west
I will stand on the shore

Take to three women
I come in with ships

Take the thrown line now
I stand in the prow

Take my morning with you
I wait to bake fishes

Stonygate

25.

Crowds cheer Eostre-morning sea on fire
Mackerel burn with gannets

Black-headed gull
Follows flame-breaker

Three cobles beach
Hot shingle hisses back

Children dance
On Vinegar Hill

26.

Suffer my children with nets
Ley on Middle Haining

From Guide Post Inn to Cherry Knowle
Nettles Lane ending Rat Hill and Howley

Nack Fields for picnics
Thristley Bank not far now

Felled Black Woods
Stephenson's gravity track

Spawn ponds
Gravel howkers

27.

At Stony Gate
On the road to Durham

Three canny women
Are skipping and singing

'We've got heads in the pot
We've got pease in the pudding

So dance with us now
Joy-days are coming'

Penshaw Monument

28.

With bells and cymbals
Ring the bounds

Lift with the bearers
Bow to the mourners

Go bare-headed
Sun-ways round

Remember to greet every reaper
On the corn-path to Pensher

29.

Pensher temple guards entrance
Waste land pylons cross over

Reliquary pieces carried to remember
Waste-tip banners and followers a faint echo

Sunset blood reflects
In meander stretch

Blue sky steel
With sharp edge hacks

30.

Ancient bairns cry ancient lament...
Templar knight caaled back from Palestine

Sybil's killing advice and warning…
Death on spiked armour

Older than John-Michael
Our shiny flawed hero

Ancient bairns
Cry ancient lament

Boldon Hill

31.

On Boldon Hill
There lived a lass

She wore a blood-red
Ribbon she wore it

Around her waist
And around her legs

About her neck
Wrapped over her face

32.

On Boldon Hill
There lived a lass

She penned a weasel
(All around the bishopric)

To nibble at words
While she sang to

Her children to dance
And unwind her

33.

On Boldon Hill
There lived a lass

She was blooded
By knowledge partly

Blinded by rigid words
She was bound facing east

She saw the good morning shepherd
Through her windings turn red

Whitburn

34.

All around the bishopric
They plough three roods they reap three roods

All around the bishopric
They yield thirty-odd shillings for cornage

All around the bishopric
They send when called their hounds to the hunt

All around the bishopric
They kiss his ringed hand

35.

Where Adam delved
The same Lord holds Esscurr

John of Whitburn
Tends forty acres

Where Eve span a weft
Between cliff and dune

Esscurr holds
Hwita's mound

36.

All around the bishopric
Uneasy goes my river girl

All around the bishopric
Uneasy goes my girl

From Hwita's mound in Boldon Book
All around the bishopric

They reap three roods they plough three roods
She rises and sails in fret from it

North Sea

37.

I can not get to my love
She's out in the cold sea

I can not touch her
She's waiting with outstretched arms

I can not see her face without kisses
I sail in an arc south-east and south-west

I set forth today and yesterday
I can not get to my love

38.

All around the white light
I will wear her old green willow

All around the channel shrouds
For twelve months and a day

And if anyone passing should ask me
The reason why I wear it now

It's O that my hinny
Is so far far away

39.

As I went out early in the
Morning of summer rising

I once met a fair hinny bird
Just as the sun did shine

What made her go out on
Her journey so brightly

She's lost over rocks all alone
In the grey blinding sea

Old Seaham

40.

Hough Foot roots touch worn sea hem
The power gone out no issue stem

Mary Mary tolls the knell
Blackthorn starlings flock farewell

Mason herringbone
Marks the north side

Come to me here
Old fisherbride fisherbride

41.

Bidders halt diesel at
Byron's walk crossing

And Seaton announcing
Another lyke crossing

To Sharpley and Burdon
And grave hillock copses

To quarry the hill
And all to me

42.

Tell her to reap it
With a sickle of leather
Dun Cow maid
Oracular time
And bind it up
With a peacock's feather
Oak runes say
She's a true love of mine

Warden Law

43.

Thorn Hill is grown under
Concrete and tar

How many tongue-ties
Will lick the honey

Thorn Hill has a crack
Full of green fossil stars

How many blinded
Will see them rise

44.

I said to the wind
Blowing crow-smoke about her

How many nest-fires
Will Spring take to come

I said to the solstice-sun
Rolling low into dark

How many yellow beaks
How many tongues

45.

Thorn Hill is set groaning
By a silver-touch finger
How many blossoms
Will pollen her quick

Thorn Hill is a black bark
Split open tomorrow-tide

How many sick mornings
Will Eskhatos bring

from MOTHERGATE

18.

Are we changed
Do we want to go further

Our minds unwound
Round the next meander

Under temple silhouette
Ten times lapped dizzy

Will we spin
To Worm Hill

To be whipped
Top to bottom

19.

We stop at the Wasteland

Fall over

Fields flattened
By apparition

No spin in us

No worm-whip wrapped round
To keep the spin going

A braked dervish
Out of touch

20.

Much ado about recognition

Worm a river child

Live aspect river

A keel way
A fluid conveyer
A man rider

A threat seen ugly
As it is now
Down the well

from ANNA MARRA MISSA

Where will you send me?
(I am in the dark places)

How many times?
(I am out of Eden now)

I draw a snake upon your back
(The tree is twisted and fruitful)

Who will put in the eye?
(The apple is blind to decide)

MORENETA

1.

Candles smoke her
Black face blacker

False-gold clothing over
Old-young shoulders

They stumble suddenly

Face to face whispers

Goaf-void prostration
Trailing behind her

Lone touching shovel

Embryo fossil hand

Polished steel

2.

Even the inverted
Mountain air shivers
With cold sun
Stored in her bed

She cups the everyday
Wordless servings

Articulate motions

Body language connections

Web over her cave
Without a centre

3.

Long lost Jordan river
Profuses her blood

Extravagant horsetail logs
Crashing to carbon

Segments dating her

A wing fan
Delicate and flattened
Wafts downdraft smoke

Brass mantlepiece pole
And velvet skirt
Drawn above blazer hand

SONG OF THE COTIA LASS

1.

The keel took my heart
In full tide it was torn
The keel took my heart
Black blood to his flame

The waggonway fall
Was braked by the river
the horse on its tether
With nose-bag and corn

The keel took my heart
To whistle and wo-lad
Down in his brig of dust
Down to his hot ash breath

2.

On lip of drift crying
I sang the raa up and down
Black the craa hinny
Ivvry day now

I sang over fell where
Grey pocked my
Green stitched hem
Smouldering sway there
Banners to brighten

The keel bought my heart
It was bonded and bound
The keel took my heart
In full tide it was torn

3.

Who rose in the morning
To see the keels row then
Who'll rise in the morning
To see the keels go

It was down by the river
Ventricles pumping there
Shute and flat bottom
Leveller schull

Who rose and who'll rise
With banners and drum thump
The keel took my heart
Silk over it laid

4.

The keel played at morning-tide
Bide and abide with me
Keel-brass for my heart blown
Banner-water bidding

Rite blinds were drawn to
Down staithe banks drawn all the way
Hats doffed and held there
In the ebb-tide hush

Down in yon forest
The keel rang my heart away
Black bells of Paradise
Hutton and Harvey change

5.

Foy-boatman blow the flame
Loosen his rope-fast sail
Scorch the wind southerly
Fill it with fire in flood

Blood rages over bar
Out in the molten toss
Fury and friend are lost days
Where you are

The keel sought my heart
In full tide it was torn
It beats every tree on fire
Wagga-pulse fossil dawn

★   ★   ★

SONG

We'll rise in the morning
To see the keels row
We'll rise in the morning
To see the keels go
We'll dance like the sun
Tid Mid Miseray
We'll dance Carlin Palm
On Paste-Egg Day

FROM

Marra Familia

(1993)

IMAGE · ARK

from IMAGE ARK

1.

My coble
Slips on
Shell sand

Oystercatchers shift

Sun-colour
Their bills rising

As morning
Squeaks in
Across water

2.

Rising and falling
My bow cuts horizon

The sun's blood
A slick dispersing

It turns into gold
It turns to silver sparkle

Seals howl out of dark
To bottle a message

5. *(Virgin of the Rocks Bay of Kotor Montenegro)*

Lady of Rocks
In your white silvered sheet

Head only uncovered

My hand is still rowing
This coble engraved
Whirlpool around you

Lady of rocks
Come out of destruction

Lady of rocks
They thorn you in roses

6.

Sand banks the haven rock
Stiff fulmar turns around

I wait for your call
In the morning

Glad Tidings ready
Wind drifting me from shore

The sun is up and going
Proud noon coming

7. SONG

Out of the haven
The bonny morning went

A wake now across water
The magic moment spent

Ripples at the sea's edge
Lapped low light farewell

Folk at the haven-house
Were ringing the morning bell

8.

I am riding
The fetch waves

Leaving morning
On their tips

When rising breezes
Cast off the froth early

Time ringing sea bells
On my sharp coble pointer

9.

But where is the figurehead
Fit for this prow

The capped dark lady
Bursting at seams

Her belly-fire
Raked down on us

Her banners in flame-light
For night and day shifters

10.

She opened herself to us
In Eden forests where she lay

We were hand in hand walking then
Like the first day forever

Flood came and went
With the moon-ark still sailing

Two by two
In and out
Where she lay

13.

Children hop hitchydabber
On her pavement Kabbala

They pitch their tin dabber
Hop up the dark tree

'Who'll bring the crown down
For Magdalene Mary

Under lamp-light
Under star-light

Who'll bring it for me'

15.

Here's a lass
With a bright thole pin

Here are the sailors
Sailing in

Here's a shepherd
Come to sing

Early in the morning

16.

Ikthus fisherman
Kissed her head

He touched her eyes
In her dreamer bed

Littoral gospeller
Saw her wed

Quite early in the swell

17.

They stood in shooting green
Early in the morning

They stood in high gold corn
Early in the day

They walked in stooked fields
Blessed are the meek ones

They gathered her cradle straw
Blessed is the day

18.

Here comes the lass
With her bright thole pin

Here come the sailors
To carry her in

A lone shepherd waits ashore
Longing to sing

Early in the morning

24.

How is her day
To be ordered
After sailing

Her farmer knows well
The colour of going...

Are all our days
Thought of then

Bindings laid bare
When the silver boat beaches

26.

Canny to me
It seemed
On our sailing

Down the sea lane
Along the dark lonnen

Land ahoy daily
Lost in
Gull noise
Each morning

Words from her hailer
Massed birds fight over

28.

Stars boundless
Yet bound to us

Guide our puny
Or momentous undertaking

Plucked fruit they seem
Plucked or about to be

Their ways are our ways
Which way the moon sails

29. SONG

Three cobles are coming
From out the deep sea
Three cobles are coming
For Elsie and me
Who'll stand in the black prow
Leading them inshore
Three cobles are coming
So sing once more sing

Three cobles are coming
With spices and gold
Coming for children
Out in the cold
Three cobles are coming
Decked red black and white
She'll stand in the black prow
Last night or tonight

31.

Five trees in Paradise…

But I do not hear
The Kingdom wind
Stirring their branches and twigs

Five trees in Paradise
Even in winter wind
From the North Sea
Or summer gusts against blue
With children jumping in it
Their coats held out

No stirring even then
And their leaves do not fall

34.

How long can I sing
The old song each morning

Red like the shepherd
Her hands raised to greet me

She spoke the words twice
And I sing in their spirit

Ship on the wind
Will it carry me with them

SONG

Will dayligone fash
Or be egged on in fettle
Its bleezer laid idle
Claes hoyed forgetten
Will neet louse its bairn
In forst heed the caaller
In hadaway neet-time
The morn's morn's nigh hand

We'll rise up aall soakin
Like babbies out o' watter
We'll gan to her gatherin
Each one a marra
We'll tack the wide lonnen
It's nee good the narra
In hadaway neet-time
When the morn's morn's nigh hand

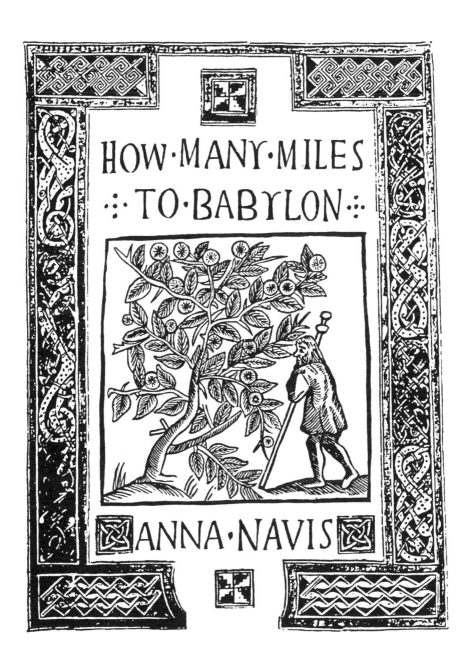

from ANNA NAVIS

SONG

How many miles to Babylon
Three score and ten
Can I get there by candlelight
Yes and back again
Here's a beck then and here's a boo
Open your gates and let us all through
Open your gates and let us all through

1.

Crowned heads rise early
In brass morning sun

Sleepers resurrected
Out of black earth

Steel rollers and bobbins
Smashed under hammer

Scrap-value line
Built over and ploughed

Only feet bring remembrance

2.

Black marra banners

Thump!

Sounding brass slowly

Thump! again

Climb the hill

Thump! the big drum goes

3.

Out of stars quickly fading
With Milky Way spilt

Blue at the rim
As the cat comes in

Stars leave to remember
Sky banners draped black

Lamped fathers rise
Out of pulley-wheel eyes

Bairns loaded on back

4.

It rises in cleft
On a dry reef remnant

Brass blare and drum thump
To her North Door knocker

Dawn limestone flora
Edge her worn pathway

Ghost rhyme remembrance
Worded by redundant men

Gathering for crack

6. SONG
Pit lie idle pit lie idle

Over stiles and up the lonnen
Saw a moose run up the waall

Up the lonnen they'll be gannin
Pit lie idle O

Soon they'll gather on the beck-side
Saw its arse and that was aall

Bait and crack and idle backsides
Pit lie idle O

7.

Black marra banners

Thump!

Sounding brass slowly

Thump! again

Climb the hill

Thump! the big drum goes

8.

She heaves
Her hip shadow
Over daylight hawthorn

Green droplet tears
Evaporate
Not ready for the beak

Steam hiss on the
Hope's steep battery sides
Cloud her eyes reading the
Morning Star's last twinkle

Soon lost between lines

12.

Here and here our Jerusalem
Is under this sun crowded

Not under unconscious collective
But all things in open bright day

Bairns touch banner hem
For power proudly winded

Our banner played
Down town-road redeemed
To candymen lost

13.

Black marra banners

Thump!

Sounding brass slowly

Thump! again

Climb the hill

Thump! the big drum goes

14.

Fellside bread brought once
To make words here

Crust-syllables syntax
Real eating for every day

Water table drinking springs
Mark scoffed lines
This noontide laid out

(Not special Sabbath words
Rumbling hungry indoors)

All tasted and shared

15.

Where is our feeding to come

The banners say know who you are
And know you must stand together

Will it come out of sky
Sun clouded with bird flight

Will it spout from the sea's edge
Shoals secretly gasping

Where is our feeding
To Tom Dick and Harry

The banners say know who you are

17.

Dreams bump into dark

Stumble-lamp under gauze veil
Lighting her face

Pick-knowledge fragmented
Stone broken-fruit offered

A roundy on fire back
Waiting to tongue
Her spitting words
They'll hook-fashion
Into mat scroll

18.

Her carpet page
Is all over us

Each stitch
A crowned head
Under fire

Feet burnish gold
To hessian bare
Of cut rags

They roll
A new ball
And roll
A new frame

The same

20.

Black marra banners

Thump!

Sounding brass slowly

Thump! again

Climb the hill

Thump! the big drum goes

21.

July trains whistle
Up a golden thread line

Past Pallion and Hylton
Only wind it all in

Through Penshaw and Sunniside
All the way into her

July trains whistle
Up a golden thread line

22.

Sooted half-grown fields
Drilled on her track sides

Half way to Dunholm
Darkening the cold green corn

Half way from seed
To golden fossil waves

Our ship steaming in

Half way to banners unfurling

Half way wind in brass

23.

They by-pass grass lovers in pollen

The dun-cow girl
Shouting a place-name

Her breasts polished yellow
His hands out of rape fields

This train awake going
And going and going there

A steamed open book
Down among gold leaf
Bold words rolled out

25.

I come with passion
At the edge

A singer
To meet me
Of the old song
Passing all comfort

Some words
Weep me
Down to you
Bones of my bones

26.

It is not
Babylon
That remains

It knocks at her
Great North Door
Thronged with
Changeling banners
And backward reading words

Songs that sound
Like the old songs
Inside out

27.

And we come in
Through corn trembling

The hiss of seed
Tinnitus overwhelming

And we come to you hinny
With waste-land banners
And fire brands

Crackling reflections
In the dark water

SONG

How many miles to Babylon

Three score and ten

Can I get there by candlelight

Yes and back again

Here's a beck then and here's a boo

Open your gates and let us all through

Open your gates and let us all through

TRIPTYCH

1. *Slogan Bread* (1–3)

Banner stitches hem them

Touched power encircled

Word issue
Their bait
Gathered round
High on fellside

Good crack yeast

Dough-rise on fender

Banners hem them encircled
Teeth sunk into slogan

2.

Loaf-tin words
Smell of rite eating

Where love begins
Crusts curl every hair

We are compressed
Into commonness

Food is for one mouth all over

Who feels the hunger pain?
No space between us

3.

Hands in oven-well ink
Make ripe golden words

Black fell IN PRINCIPIO
Our corn-sickle inscription

Cut green-vellum grass
And stretched
Cow parsley haze

Words broken to mouth
On a table before us

FROM

Lammas Alanna

(2000)

AFOREWORD

1.

Dorado full sky
Reflects in her water

Naked verbum immersed
But coming again to us
With words and the gab
Made golden

It is a cry
Out of beginning

A seed to the harvest reaped

A heart-beat
Of the spoken

2.

Swim internal
Seed implanted
Noisy workings
All the while

Then come the stirrings
Dark Eden expanding
First out of Ark
In deluge to dry land

A deep rooted tree
And dove-guide
Through stress land
With promise of
Foothold made hold

3.

A nativity accentor
Sings in the branches

It is word-flesh music
Heard first early morning

Giving praise
At the wonder
Of her bright
Herald star

A sign of beginning
A spuggie testament

FIRSTGATE

So now yer knaa how aall the folks on byeth sides o' the Wear lost lots o' sheep and lots o' sleep and lived in m'tal fear... so let's hev one to brave Sor John that kept the bairns from harm... saved coos and calves by makkin halves of the famous Lambton Worm

MORT TIAMAT

Remember me O remember me said Tiamat. I am our dream for all living and dying. I am the seed in the ground and the shoot and the harvest. Come gather together when the moon is a sickle and the field is a golden sea. But the LORD *spread out his net to enfold her*

> He called up the evil wind
> He let it loose in her face
>
> When she opened her mouth
> Fierce wind filled her belly
>
> Her body was distended
> And her mouth wide open
>
> He bent back his bow
> And released a great arrow
>
> It cut into her side
> Splitting the heart
>
> She struggled for life
> But soon it was gone
> He stood on her carcass
>
>
> The Lord
> Stamped on the legs
> Of Tiamat
>
> With his unmerciful hammer
> He crushed her skull
>
> When the arteries
> Had been cut

The North Wind
Bore them away

He heaped up a mountain
Over Tiamat's head

He formed hills
On her breasts

He pierced them to make rivers

Her tail he bent
Across the sky

A Milky Way remembrance

Remember me

Her voice
Cried over the waters

Remember me

She thundered
In the sky

Remember me

She gasped in the black rock
Crushed underground

Remember me

In the Spring of the World

PSALM

I went into my lost love's place
Our Eden is enchanter and golden rod

I ate the fruit
Of my lost love's death

Our Eden is Devil's bit
And smooth sow thistle

I spat out the seed
Like Solomon's seal

Our Eden is Mountain everlasting
And small fleabane

I touched the pale root
Of my lost love's face

Our Eden is Tree of Heaven
And pellitory of the wall

QUEST

It is a Cockerooso hop

A singing interlaced path

A long way to Tipperary myth

A hardness of the heart
We struggle with

A self and other selves

Not one without the other

A Jack shine the Maggi to follow

A Bethlehem harvest now

✣HEAVENFIELD✣

I · JOHNBIRD

images found in and around the book of wearmouth

LIGHTKNIFE · cuts
cake-dark hole
gobbling us and pandect
figures painted along
shore say that from
✝ beach-gloom of the
codex there is no end ·:·
no end to spuggie
swallow after hall
and solstice struggle
no morning in the
morning they say

2.

Day faces west gazing in majesty

Throne stool ringing
Four khaki walkers
And humming flyers

With pink under grey clouds
Even now true

And uncials beginning and end
Old and new together

3.

This lot we plodge

Barefoot Evangelist's eagle
Our wing over grey swell

For now we see
Horizon cliff and cave mist

And pebbles turning forever
To beach dust

Clinging between toe's print
And infilling ingrown
His nail-pain washes away

6.

Dark in thorn tree dark
Birds blossom

Its spikes winter bares
His night thoughts
Roost among them
A shufflinflg nocturne ritual

But who is here
And the Lord risen

7.

He whispers behind us
When bank gravity
Lightens our step

And dark increases
Our going over the hill

He is shadow maker
Even in shadow

He is dream light
We hardly grasp on waking

His memory
Squeezing out of hand
As we grope
Heads jarping Easter in our ears

9.

I will spitfire
The counted sparrow heads

And rake
Mustard seed fields
I Johnbird

With winged Matthew man
And look
Lion flyer leaping bull force

MAY TIME

from the Black Book of Carmarthen

Kintevin
Maytime
Fairest season

Yoked oxen plough the furrow
The sea is green reflecting
Fresh colours clothe the earth

When cuckoos sing on fine tree tops
My sadness grows

Fire-smoke stings

At night I am restless
Since my loved ones have gone

On hill and in hollow
On islands of the sea
Everywhere you go
With the White Christ
There is no place forsaken

Seven saints
Seven score
And seven hundred
Have gone with the White Christ

There is no dread there

A favour I ask
Please do not refuse me

May I have peace
May I find the gateway to Glory
Among Christ's people I should not be sad

SCORDIE

1.

Plain hermit Cuthbertus
In east end splendour

Bede outside the
Blocked west door

Carved Apocalypse words
His Morning Star Christ

Crucified upended Peter
On faint Galilee fresco

The old fisherman
Ladder top at foot
fixed with Roman nails

2. *(Amiatinus)*

Three times fivehundred beast skins
To a slaughter of pandect

Sixhundred his crossbrood
Kiss farewell

CEOLFRIDIS ANGLORUM
EXTREMIS DEFINIBAS ABBAS

The desert movement
Smudges ink here

fingers will not write
For northern winter

3.

Lion-flame eaten
In Tunc-page Kells

Virgin folio like
Cuthbert's oak

But viridian and purple
Not simply incised

Saintly profiles in box frame
Jewelled dog-head seat

Angels with the
Look of Donovan

4.

Echternach's Lion Mark
Leaps after fledgling

Chad's carpet writhes
Like a stone turned over

Out of tangled genealogy
Kell's Jesse sprouts

INITIUM blossoming

CHIRO full grown

5.

Durrow beasts in interlace
Bite cased Wearmouth stone

Pictish manuscript-slabs
Thumbed by all weather

Gospel book 'fashioned for
God and Saint Cuthbert

And all the saints
In Lindisfarne'

Orange relic sun
Crossbrood trooping west

6.

Durham Gospel fragment
Matthew's ending recto through skin

Crucifixion in A.II.17
Interlace confusing angels

And spear bearer
And sponge bearer

Are my burning eyes
(Folio thirty eight)

The Lord's last flare
Fading on vellum

EXILE

At the ferrystones I left them

Their river-wrinkle
Showed no reflection
Of vessel and grey band gathered

Only gold of the cross glowed
Brood all around it
Not a hand said farewell
When my ship-drift
Sought the break-white bar-gap

Now it is Friday and the fishers beach
Hauled out headland seals
Wail in blue before chanters

I am over rock and across sand
An exile white beyond the bar

THE SEAFARER

I tell a true story
A tale of myself

Sitting all day at the oars
Gripping against sorrow

In bitterness I steered my coble
Among endless cares

Bows through tossed foam
Watching for cliffs
Numbed with night falling

☦

Sea-weary
Cares hungered my heart

Cold gnawed at my feet

No happy man can guess on land
How I wandered without kin
Marraless in frost

☦

There was bitter hail
And sea birds' lonely call

Not men's laughter
Gathered together

But gannet splash

Sharp beak in my heart despairing

✢

With friendship
Life is sweet

Warm around hearth
They barely think
Of the banished man

At nightfall
Weary at sea
In snow from the north

✢

Thoughts come knocking
Of a great sea crossing

Again the mind moves
Soul seeks the way

Over wind-water fetch
To new people far off

✢

No man is so wise
Before going
Who does not think over
Where the Lord leads him now

Not dwelling on trinkets
But her delights put aside
Only sea-waves in eyesight
Salt tears at her loss

✣

Green forests and farms
Communities thriving

Urge the eager to voyage
To fells fresh growth

Where the cuckoo calls
Herald of summer

But sorrows still throng
In the midst of his song

✣

What happy man can know
What hardships come
Who sail in spray
Far from land

The cuckoo's sound
Drags me across water

I remember the Lord's kindness

I do not believe
Earthly things
Are everlasting

Three things threaten our peace

Illness or age or vengeance
Shall draw the breath

But praise well won is lasting

Men and angels shall honour it

On good lips it shall not die

✢

Days are soon over
When a leader fails

There are none like those
Whose good deeds
Were the World's first

Our songs honoured them

But excellence grows old

Age greys and thins the head

We cannot lift a finger

It is no good laying
Up treasures on earth

That cannot allay
The Judgement of God

✢

BEDE'S GOING

Migrating wings take him

I inked these flat birds
Like Lindisfarne pages
After gifting his Cuthbert book

I was there
I took the north lonnen
Waded Don then at ebbtide

Had I heard they said
Only hours since he worked
And hours to that journey
All must make

'No man is so wise
Before going
Who does not think over
What good or evil
His soul will be judged'

He said

SIX ISLAND SUNSET

1.

Blue-eyed Evangelist
You came in skins
To this treeless island

Jack Eagle Evangelist
You roost
A stone bird now

The beginning word
You brought
Is lapidary light

Green lichen
Gems cold pictish boss
Unforbidden child on the cross

2.

West kindles beatitude
The earth shall inherit

It was before the fire
Brendan left ring of saintly pebbles

His footstep dissolved
His keel deep in shingle

But the heretic sunset burns
Rack centuries southward

3.

Paul with stone head
Wept long for his brother

The Lord of sunset
Is taking names

A star-maiden's foot
Dances on water

We call her Bridie
The white daughter

4.

They welcome fiery angel

Virus sword of all horizons

Lord give us this day

Their parliament discusses
fish eggs and sheep
Who sink or swim with common boat

5.

Returning again
She spoke out of currah

Blue net from her mouth

The crowd stood with dunlin
And weed jumble

Words garbled in surf

6.

High golden star
Between my eyes
St Kilda burns
Be wise be wise

High golden star
Cold Pentecost tongue
She burns afar
The sea is dumb

High golden star
Who speaks for men?
The west is red
Amen Amen

DREAMRISE

MIDWINTER SONG

1.

Longshore Feneris rives

Gale splits on groin

White curtain drench

Bricks and flint
Sheep and goats
Granite in the teeth

Stand up
The storm
Unleashes
Counting

2.

Remember the kiss
Of first rain before Ragnarok

A lark in meadow grass
And flowers
Her hair almost covered

Pollen-nose
And buttercup reflection
Yellow cheek

3.

He said the meek
Would inherit

Stood there
On this hill
Where his mother
Met a stranger
From Hope Wood

And he met another
That first summer

4.

And the blessed thing
Won't lie down

It won't lie down
Stars finally witness

Even the moon
In its last dying
Testifies Bethlehem

5.

I will go and no more
Said wince to sickle
I will go and no more
Said cry to wind
I will go and no more
Said deep wound to throbbing
I will go and no more
Said hurt to steel

6.

This back end
May be the last

Have you seen my
Bonny lad limping

Last year's child
His ear now close to earth
Waiting the first squeak of green

7.

Are you coming
To the woodbine
To the nip
The drag
The swallow

Are you coming
To the nettle
To the blister
Pain and rue

Are you coming
To the kissing
To the sorrel
Dock and yarrow

Are you coming
Adam handed
To her cree-play
Eden school

8.

I do not wish
The moon to lag
Come to the fields

Or the sun to
Sleep the caller
Come with your poppy-flood

I do not wish the
Cock to un-crow
Over dyked barley

9.

Farmer farmer
May we cross your golden river
May we cross your golden river
In our silver boat?

I will call out the colour
Of the one who'll cross my river
Who will cross my golden river
In that silver boat

from **In Easthope**

2.

Clouds appear
Over the head of the hill

Blue is going I heard it said

Wrinkles soon darken
The brow watching

And blue is broken

Cracked patches of it falling
Till nothing
Nothing remains but cloud
At the head of the hill
And waste broken blue
Lying in the fields
Surrounding

3.

The dying blossom in heaps
Like dead flowers cast away

Red and white blossoms

And the sea shivers light
On its rippled surface
Over to islands
Those black islands
Looking into the sun

The same sun that
Rises and sets on us

And her flesh is soft
Under the arm
Next to her breast

5.

Always when new rain
Bursts its droplets
Against glass

Or is felt tapping flesh
To trickle and be smeared

Always then I should remember
How it seemed to fall free
Returning to us

6.

From once a mill hill
Mist hides hollows
And orange ball is half in haze

Barley wet sunset
Cream snail crossing road
Over spilt blue pattern of paint

No scarecrow's tattered wooden cross
No ghost-red sails
At pylon's end

8.

Crows I saw
And may dying

But summer sang naked
And wind
Barely a breeze
Warmed her waist
Till I came

When sentinel beeches
Stood west of us

And rust nestled in blossom

from *IMAGES FROM SAMUEL PALMER*

1. *The magic apple tree*

I walked in this valley
Of the magic apple tree

I talked to a piping shepherd
Stooked corn tumbling down

I ate a red apple there
Full branches bending over

I touched the steeple pointer
Gold-tipped among barton ricks

2. *Cornfield by moonlight with evening star*

Waning moon
Touches the corn
Ablaze now

Scribbled hills
Her breasts uncovered

I walk the path
Between
With staff and dog

A star overhead
Comes through cloud
To follow

3. *Harvest moon Shoreham*

He stands with arms outstretched
As the others stoop

Greeting the haloed moon
Resting on a wooded bank and cliff

Purple sky and massed leaves
Nestle the red roofed
Church and steeple

Strewn corn is on the ground
Thrown after their sickle-arm sweeping

6. *Early morning*

They huddle under a tree in corn
Our ancient children waiting

Yellowing eastern sky
Pushes her shadow
Across grass and rocks

A hare boxes the dark back

A dandelion clock
Waits for her morning lip breath

He loves me not

He loves me not

He loves

BAIRNSEED

BAIRNSEED

*These twenty-six streets were within the wall
of the original mining village of Silksworth*

1.

Aline Lord Robert
Quarry Maria Hill

Remember the evictions there
In eighteen ninety-one

Remember the candymen
Slipping the greasy stairs

Remember the cayenne pepper
As they moved their bits o' things

2.

Londonderry Silksworth Terrace
Split by the school

Girls in the west black yard
Eastern side lads bool

On the mountain stands a lady
Skip the turning rope you two

Mountykitty one
Leap one two three
Mountykitty mountykitty
Fall off me

3.

Edward Stewart Frances
Doctor Hopper's bones

Run down the black path
Keep ahead of stones

Baked bread on window-sills
Flat-cake fadge and loaf

A whole street of baking days
Draws bairns by the nose

4.

Cornelia Tempest Vane
Twin middens across the road

Precious loves and prize leeks
In black garden soil grown

Vane Arms for argument
Maughin's shop alone

Glass-ally kids in back lane
Making their way home

5.

Castlereagh Tunstall
Wynyard William John

West end and east end
All within the wall

Fish shop and cropper
Beasts to their fall

Father brings us chocolate
From the I.O.G.T. Hall

6.

Seaham West Henry
Charles North Mary George

Mother's chapel my chapel
Say my 'piece' rehearsed

Grandmother Mary
And Grandmother Jane

Big Meeting banners
Coming up the lane

from SONG

1.

We meet at the lamp
And watch the moon
The end of the world
Is coming soon

CHORUS
What shall we play
On Vinegar Hill
Hitchydabber say Hollycarrside
Let's hoist the banner
Let's mountykitty
Let's skip let's tig
Let's dress the bride

2.

Mam's got Jesus
Dad's got Marx
Eve's got me
In the wash-house dark

CHORUS
What shall we play
On Vinegar Hill
Hitchydabber say Hollycarrside
Let's hoist the banner
Let's mountykitty
Let's skip let's tig
Let's dress the bride

3.
Don't knock the props
Off Armstrong's wall
He'll clip yer lugs
And keep yer ball

CHORUS
What shall we play
On Vinegar Hill
Hitchydabber say Hollycarrside
Let's hoist the banner
Let's mountykitty
Let's skip let's tig
Let's dress the bride

4.
Mackerel Mackerel
From out the deep sea
Don't follow Polaris
To Elsie and me

CHORUS
What shall we play
On Vinegar Hill
Hitchydabber say Hollycarrside
Let's hoist the banner
Let's mountykitty
Let's skip let's tig
Let's dress the bride

SONG

As aa was gannin
Through Chester-le-Street
Three canny women
Were mackin a feast
They had a stew-pot full
It bubbled and squeaked
As aa was gannin
Through Chester-le-Street

As aa was gannin
Through Houghton-le-Spring
The same three women
Were hevin a fling
They louped ower dyke tops
With a kite on a string
As aa was gannin
Through Houghton-le-Spring

As aa was gannin
Through Pelton Fell
Three bonny women
Were ringing a bell
A cat with a fiddle
Was up a-high singin
As aa was gannin
Through Pelton Fell

As aa was gannin
Through Hetton-le-Hole
Bairns were dippin
Their crusts in a bowl
The women kept fillin it
Aall the time fillin
As aa was gannin
Through Hetton-le-Hole

As aa was gannin
To old Durham town
The three canny women
Were dancing around
With skirts out like banners
As bold as brass sound
As aa was gannin
To old Durham town

from HIS BRIGHT SILVER

(SONG)
Traditional

The bonny pit laddie
The canny pit laddie
The bonny pit laddie for me O

He sits on his cracket
And hews in his jacket
And brings the bright silver to me O

1.

Pit yackers dance to
Pulley-wheel buzzer

At Kelloe the calf hill
Chipped cross-face of Helen

At Hetton and Elemore
Trimdon and Esh

Little Chance is the gallowa
Putters all bless

2.

Beech candles drip wax
Into root-fibre cutting

Full draped bier
Draws empty one up

On twisted steel rope
On gravity bobbins

As children whirl haloes
Discarded hemp-core lit

4.

Brick warren estate
Rabbit Wood overrun

High rise shadow blade
Has steel cord cut

Ghostly crossing keeper
Muffler clay pipe and spit

Old 'face' now 'bank man'
Like Hefænricaes Uard
Dreams and puffs his twist

6.

Memorial words
Uncial Quarter seam

Bonny May morning
Night shift on the face

Telltale yellow cagebird
First shift in the Gate poor lads

Black explosion banner
Stone names all but one

7.

Candles flicker in eviction tents
What Kingdom without common feasting

When they were seated
Silk banners on fellside

Friends after nettle broth
Turned slogans into bread

By the poor for the poor
They taught themselves

8.

Street children cry Cockerooso
Generations hop across

Spuggie chorus crack
Cathedral choir sing anthem

'Our feet shall stand
In thy gates O Jerusalem'

Larks rise with brass
Big Meeting last one for Eden

9.

The bonny pit laddie
Sits on his cracket

Corf fill the keel
Keel fill the brig

Dark drift or shaft hole
He hews in his jacket

And brings the bright silver
The canny pit laddie

His eye full of silver to me

SONG

A Wearside version

It's O but aa ken well
Ah you hinny bird
The bonny lass of Pennywell
Ah you Ah
She's lang-haired and bonny-fyaced
Ah you hinny bird
With gold and silver on her breast
Ah you Ah

Hetton line comes ower the top
Ah you hinny bird
Waggons bound for Lambton Drop
Ah you Ah
Peter's for owld Bede
Ah you hinny bird
Chapelgarth sunk in a field
Ah you Ah

There's Pans Bank for salters
Ah you hinny bird
And Hope race-track for halters
Ah you Ah
Hendon for taarytowt
Ah you hinny bird
And Silksworth pit for 'aall out'
Ah you Ah

There's Backhouse for artists
Ah you hinny bird
And Old Vic pub for Chartists
Ah you Ah
There's Roker front for bonny lights

Ah you hinny bird
Jack's Maggi shine for dark nights
Ah you Ah

There's Tunstall Hills for Maiden Paps
Ah you hinny bird
With lovers lying in the grass
Ah you Ah
There's Tid Mid and Miseray
Ah you hinny bird
Carlin Palm and Paste-Egg-Day
Ah you Ah

There's Doxfords and Pickersgills
Ah you hinny bird
Riveter's and plater's skills
Ah you Ah
There's collier brigs and keel row
Ah you hinny bird
All gone out in the big tide flow

Ah you Ah

from DURHAM BEATITUDE

The Easington Colliery disaster in 1951
remembered at the Durham Miners' Gala

1.

Gorse blazing on clifftop
I saw three ships
Thorns and May blossom
Explosion at pit

Saul's Dead March
Common grave and grief
Beatitude their banner
Weeping and drum beat

A gentleness flowered
In each drum silence
A Kingdom confronted
Each green thorn

They that mourn
Came here in July
Field blessed with banners
Thronged comforting hush

I saw three ships
Through the gorse sail in
They came to Death's harvest
They came to pulley-wheels

5.

Pulley-wheel eyes
Haul ships

White elder sing
Psalms rust to berry

Who sows in tears
Reaps in joy

Clifftop ritual
Picnic-Haggadah

Crushed-Magdalene oil
Gorse-golden-vessels

Here and here
Is Jerusalem

Three ships beach
On shingle spoil

Notes

NOTES

from CRACKNRIGG (1983)

from Hen Meneu (30)

Part 1. *Genizah*: '(The contents of) a storeroom for damaged, discarded, or heretical manuscripts and sacred relics , usu. attached to a synagogue' (OED).

Part 3. *Eloi:* Christ's last cry on the Cross 'Eloi, Eloi, lema sabachthani?' (My God, My God, why hast thou forsaken me?) Mark 15.34.

Part 5. *Maiden Paps*: old name for Tunstall Hills, limestone outcrops on the edge of Sunderland overlooking WM's house, Easthope. They have a significant place in WM's poetry as part of what might be thought of as a ritual landscape that he read into the geography surrounding his home.

Part 6. *'yem*: home

Part 7. *maggi light*: 'From the children's game "Jack shine the Maggi (or light)". This was a most mysterious game, played in the dark. The children divided into two groups. One group went off into the dark with a torch or lantern, the purpose being to find the group with the light. When the pursuers shouted "Jack shine the Maggi" the light had to be switched on briefly. The holders of the light then moved on and hid somewhere else. I like to think that the Maggi is derived from the Magi who followed the star.'
Cockerooso: 'A popular game when I was a boy. One of the children stood in the middle of the road while the others gathered on one pavement. The middle kid called on one of the gathering to try to hop across the road, the aim being to prevent this by shoulder-charging. If a foot was put down that person stayed in the middle to help. If the hopper got across he or she would shout "Cockerooso" and all the others then hopped across. After a while the game got rather boisterous as the sides were evened up.'

Crist Gwyn (34)

Part 1. *Cyntefin:* Maytime (Welsh).

The Even Ships (37)

Part 1. *Wednesday Singers:* the folk club of the Elliotts of Birtley, an important folk dynasty. WM visited regularly with his friend, the poet Roger Garfitt.

Thorn Hill nuns: the Little Sisters of the Poor had a house in the Thornhill area of Sunderland. 'For many years I walked from my home near Tunstall Hills (Maiden Paps) past Thorn Hill, where there was a Convent of Mercy, to my work at a local hospital.' [WM's notes to *Hinny Beata*]

Jock-o-the-pit: Jock Purdon, miner and communist singer-songwriter and regular performer at the Elliotts' club. See *The Echo of Pit Boots, Pitwork, Politics & Poetry: The collected songs and poems of Jock Purdon* (The Common Trust/Northern Voices, undated).

Part 2. *XPI*: or 'Chi-rho' – Greek contraction of Christ's name often seen in religious imagery. WM probably had in mind the famous Chi-Rho page at the opening of the Gospel of Matthew in the Lindisfarne Gospels

Part 3. *Hollycarrside and Vinegar Hill*: to the north and south sides of Tunstall Hills.

Hitchydabber: a North-East name for hopscotch.

Mountykitty: another children's game. One team forms a kind of linear scrum against a wall or post; the other take turns to leap-frog over the rearmost and bounce to the front of the 'kitty'. When all are mounted, they bounce up and down crying 'Mounty-kitty, mountykitty one, two three!' If the kitty remains standing, that side has won. WM, in the course of a project with Gateshead schools, taught the game to junior schoolchildren. The game was immediately stopped by an alarmed headmaster.

The Round Dance (39)

Part 2. *Coble:* a traditional North-East open-topped fishing boat. The 'o' is pronounced 'oh' on the Northumberland and Durham coast.

The Bald Ship (41)

Sair Fyel'd Hinny: an old traditional North-East song in which an old man addresses an oak tree. *Sair:* sorely. *F'yeld:* failed.

Part 1. *Cariadwen:* The white Goddess (Welsh).
Callerherrin: Fresh (as opposed to smoked or salted) herring.

Part 3. *Mabyn:* Cornish saint, daughter of Welsh king.

Part 4. *Kyo, Esh:* Villages in Co. Durham

from **A19 Hymn** (44)

Down in Yon Forest etc: the opening lines of *The Corpus Christi Carol*.

Part 6. *Four for kestrel... pandect-calf... winged cat... angel-man*: WM's take on the traditional images for the four Evangelists (the eagle for St John, the ox for St Luke, the lion, usually shown with wings, for St Mark, the angel for St Matthew. He may have had in mind the image of the Evangelists surrounding the figure of Christ in the *Codex Amiatinus*, the Gospel book created at the Wearmouth-Jarrow monastery in the late 7th/early 8th century. See the Library of Congress *Codex Amiatinus*, image 1591.

from **Kildan Fragments** (47)

Part 5. *Conachair:* The highest summit on Hirta, the main island of St Kilda.

Marratide (50)

Marratide: one of WM's compound coinings: the time or season of the marra, 'equal, like, comrade, friend, workmate'. [WM's notes to *Hinny Beata*]

Part 1. *Backscrubbed blue scars:* miners, especially those working in thin seams, acquired a series of scars along their protruding veterbrae.

Part 5. *Crake-men:* men 'appointed by the Union Lodge...to go round the village (Silksworth) with a "crake" or rattle calling men to meetings' [WM's notes to *Hinny Beata*]

Dunholm: early name for the headland on which Durham was founded. Its use so close to mention of Cuthbert indicates than WM intended the reader to make a link between the journey to Durham for the miners' gala, and the travels of the community of Cuthbert as they found a final resting place for his coffin.

Haugh: a river-meadow partially surrounded by a meander.

from HINNY BEATA (1987)

from Malkuth (54)

'The poem is based on a walk from Sunderland to Durham with a friend, Gordon Brown, on Midsummer Day, along old railway tracks and waggonways.' [WM's notes to *Hinny Beata*]

Malkuth: Hebrew – 'Kingdom', one of WM's key terms. 'I don't mean Heaven: some special thing happening; maybe it didn't last forever, but it was always the moving towards it, not maybe not actually reaching, but moving towards it' (interview with Gordon D. Brown). See also *Marradharma*.

Corve: 'Large Basket or container used for transporting coal.' [WM's notes to *Hinny Beata*]

Tyup/Tup: 'The Tup in question was the last corve of coal that was drawn from the pit at the end of the year, which was buss'd or dressed with lighted candles previous to leaving the bottom of the shaft.' From a footnote to Matthew Tate's poem 'Thi Bussen ov thi Tyup'. [WM's notes to *Hinny Beata*]

1. *Goaf:* the unsupported area left after the coal face advanced, often left to collapse, leading to land-subsidence above (see section 5). For an exhaustive account of miners' terminology or pitmatic see: Bill Griffiths, *Pitmatic: the Talk of the North-East Coalfield* (Northumbria University, 2007).

2. *Mothergate:* The main roadway through a mine.

Putter's Curse: The putter pushed full tubs of coal from the coal-face to where they could be transported by engine. Usually a young man who had not graduated to hewing.

Little Chance: The name of a pit-pony in a comic song of the same title. WM frequently uses such sources in a 'straight faced' manner that subtly modulates the emotional tone of fundamentally serious poems.

6. *Eskhatos:* Greek, 'last.' Here appears to refer to the catastrophic end of a mine, but is also the root of the term 'eschtalogical' – the theological study of the 'last things', contrasting with 'Genesis' in section 1.

11. *If I rise with sheep...*: Old North-East song 'Bonny at Morn'.

13. *1822 line:* The railway designed by George Stephenson and engineered by his son, Robert. See Jake Morris-Campbell's introduction for the walk route that WM and his close friend and activist Gordon D. Brown (GDB) devised along this and other disused lines.

16. *Cuthbert's...high resting place:* Tradition has it that the last resting-place of Cuthbert's coffin before it finally rested in Durham was at Warden Law, a hill between Sunderland and Houghton-le-Spring overlooking the North-East coastline, a stopping-off point on WM's & GDB's route to Durham.

17. *Haliwirfolc:* 'Holy man people' – the Anglo-Saxon community of St Cuthbert.

18. *Striking Miners/ Riddling for coal:* WM and GDB encountered striking miners doing this in the embankment of the 1822 railway

when walking to Durham during the miners' strike of 1984-85.

35. *Nystagmus/ Pulley-wheel eyes:* the image derives from the opposite directions of rotation of the dual winding-wheels at the pit-head. Nystagmus was also a common ailment among miners 'triggered by returning to daylight after the poor lighting underground' (Bill Griffiths, *Pitmatic: the Talk of the North-East Coalfield* (Northumbria University, 2007). WM's own father was forced to retire from pit work because of the condition.

Hidden of the foot: Job, chapter 28, verses 1-11 describe mining, and are inscribed on the Miners' Memorial in Durham Cathedral. See also section 40.

37. *Coming Doon the Waggon Way:* Traditional song, sometimes known as 'Clap Hands for Daddy'.

47. *Worm river-bend etc:* Refers to the course of the River Wear at Durham winding around the site of the main meeting field of the Miners' Gala. Here and elsewhere in WM's poetry it indicates the Lambton Worm (pr. as in 'dorm'), a monster that terrorised medieval Wearside. As elsewhere in his choice of sources, he sets up a tension between the seriousness of his imagery and the main source, which is a comic retelling of the tale usually attributed to C.M. Leumane written for a pantomime in the late 19th century.

Wiramutha Helix (65) [all from WM's Notes to *Hinny Beata*]

For many years I walked from my home near Tunstall Hills (Maiden Paps) past Thorn Hill, where there is a Convent of Mercy, to my work at a local hospital. Looking at a map one day I realised that there were a number of major features around the town that were four miles from a centre at Thorn Hill, e.g. Warden Law, which is connected with the Dun Cow Legend and is reputed to be the last resting place of Saint Cuthbert before Durham. From this grew the idea of the Helix, to include further historic and geographical sites.

Worm: The Lambton Worm.

Cotia: Harraton Colliery – after Nova Scotia, because so many Scotsmen worked there.

Reef (Maiden Paps): The remains of a barrier reef which extended down the east Durham coast.

Hope House: House in the valley.

Crake Man: The man appointed by the Union Lodge who used to go round the village (Silksworth) with a 'crake' or rattle calling the men to meetings.

Shakey-Down: A bed made up on the floor.

Marra: Equal, like, comrade, friend, work-mate.

Hastings Hill: There is a re-constructed Bronze Age burial kist from Hastings Hill in Sunderland Museum. At the time of writing this was on the top floor, and on the stairs leading to it is a 15th-century wooden Virgin and Child.

Moses: The horned head of Moses is the crest on the east face of Hylton Castle, home of the famous ghost, the Caad Lad of Hylton.

Twined Serpents: These are carved on the porch doorway of St Peter's church Monkwearmouth, founded AD 674.

Coble or cobble: A fishing boat.

Leningrad: A copy of Bede's *History* now in Russia.

Pensher Temple: The classical temple-monument erected on Penshaw Hill in 1844, to commemorate John Lambton the first Earl of Durham.

John-Michael: An earlier John Lambton was the slayer of the Lambton Worm.

Boldon Book: The Domesday Book of the north, initiated by Bishop Hugh du Puiset in 1183.

Byron's Walk: A lane named after the poet Lord Byron who was married in the hall nearby.

from **Mothergate** (87)

18. *Temple silhouette:* The Penshaw Monument, an imitation of the Theseum at Athens and standing above the Wear to the south, is a prominent hilltop landmark in east Co. Durham.

18. *Worm Hill:* As noted above, a major source re the Lambton Worm is Leumane's song. In it, the Worm 'wraps its tail ten times roond Pensha' Hill'. Local tradition, however, specifies the much smaller Worm Hill on the north bank of the river near Fatfield.

20. *A keel way:* Keels were river-boats that carried coal from riverside staithes at the end of wagonways leading from the mines, to load collier ships in the deep water at river mouths.

Moreneta (89)

Moreneta: The black Madonna of Monserrat.

Out of Eden: Apart from the obvious reference to the Genesis story and the tradition of the Virgin Mary as a 'second Eve', WM had in mind the parallel between coal and the blackened wooden madonna figure as well as Castle Eden near the Durham coast.

Song of the Cotia Lass (91)

Cotia: 'For many years Harraton Colliery was known as "Cotia Pit". This was because of the large number of Scottish people working there, who had migrated south for work.' Sitelines Newcastle website.

from **MARRA FAMILIA** (1993)

from **Image Ark** (97)

31. *Five Trees of Paradise:* from the Gnostic Gospel of Thomas verse 19: 'For there are five trees for you in Paradise which remain undisturbed summer and winter and whose leaves do not fall. Whoever becomes acquainted with them will not experience death.' (tr. Thomas O. Lambdin)

Song (108)

Dayligone: daybreak.

Bleezer: blazer, a metal plate held in front of a kindled fire to 'bleeze it up'.

Claes hoyed: clothes thrown.

Neet louse: night, lose.

Forst: first.

heed the caaller: 'caaler' could be 'fresh' as in callerherrin', but the use of the double 'a' suggests the act of caalin' (calling), hence: heed the 'knocker-up' telling the miner it's time to rise for his shift.

***from* Anna Navis** (108)

A typical piece of WM's David Jones-like naming. *Navis:* Latin, ship. The poem centres on the annual Miners' Gala at Durham, which Anne Stevenson noted as 'for him, the climactic point of the year'. 'Anna' may therefore a feminised form of 'annus' to give the sense: 'the (feminine) ship of the year'.

14. *Fellside bread etc:* 'After the strike had continued for some time, and the men and their families were in consequence suffering from the effects of hunger, it was suggested that every man attending the meeting from the pits which were still at work, and could afford it, should bring a loaf of bread to the meeting. This caused a great attraction, and the meeting was very numerously attended. Hundreds of loaves were laid out in the field, and were formed into letters making the texts: – "Go thou and do likewise" "a friend in need is a friend indeed" "help one another".' Richard Fynes: *The Miners of Northumberland and Durham*, 1873. Epigraph to Triptych, Left Side, *Cracknrigg*. See also 'Slogan Bread' in this volume.

Roundy: 'a large coal'. Richard Oliver Heslop, *Northumberland Words. A Glossary of words used in the county of Northumberland*

and on Tyneside (English Dialect Society/Keegan Paul Trench, Turner & Co, London, 1892).

Hook-fashion...carpet page: Here WM is likening the great non-figurative pages of e.g. the Lindisfarne Gospels to the domestic folk-tradition of making 'proggy' or rag-mats.

Slogan Bread (121)

See above note to 'Anna Navis'.

1. *Good crack:* 'light talk, conversation, boasting' (Heslop, ibid). 'Crack' was long in North-East usage long before the Gaelic 'craic' became more fashionable. First citations are of late 16th and early 17th centuries, predating the influx of Irish workers to North-East industries.

3. IN PRINCIPIO: 'In principio erat Verbum', 'In the beginning was the Word', the first words of St John's Gospel. WM has in mind one of the great pages of the Lindisfarne Gospels.

from LAMMAS ALANNA (2000)

Lammas: 'First day of August, formerly observed as a harvest festival, from Old English *hlāfmæsse*, loaf-mass.' OED

Mort Tiamat (128)

'In Babylonian myth the Great Goddess Tiamat was destroyed by the God Marduk.' [WM's notes to *Lammas Alanna*]

Psalm (130)

Out of Eden: WM's imagery often dwelt on the denes – steep-sided wooded valleys – of the Durham coastline, Castle Eden Dene being a prominent example.

from I John Bird (134)

See note to 'A19 Hymn' above; 'Four for kestrel' etc.

7. *Heads Jarping Easter:* along with paste-egg rolling at Easter, jarping was a traditional children's contest whereby hard-boiled eggs would be jabbed against one another with the aim of cracking an opponent's shell before one's own

Scordie (139)

'Cuthbertus/ In east end splendour... Bede outside / the blocked west door': The relative position of the two saints' tombs in Durham cathedral.

Amiatinus: See note to 'A19 Hymn' above.

Midwinter Song (153)

Hope Wood: Hope is a north-country word for an upland valley.

'Farmer farmer/ May we cross your golden river': another reference to one of WM's childhood street games. The 'Farmer' tries to catch a nominated individual as they cross the 'river' (the street); if that person succeeds in crossing, all the rest rush over at once.

Bairnseed (163)

1. *Candymen:* Bailiffs or bailiffs' hired men, often, as here, evicting striking miners from their tied cottages

2. *Mountykitty:* See note on 'The Even Ships'.

5: I.O.G.T.: the Independent Order of Good Templars.

from **His Bright Silver** (170)

Song. *Crackit:* A low stool used by miners while hewing, either to sit or to lean on when working under a lower roof.

1. *Chipped cross-face of Helen:* The Romanesque Kelloe Cross is to be found in the Norman church of St Helen, Kelloe, Co. Durham. The sculptured designs describe the finding of the 'true cross' by St Helena in Jerusalem. [WM notes to *Lammas Alanna*]

2. *Full draped bier etc:* WM is describing a gravity line in which coal-laden trucks bound for the staithes were connected via pulleys at the head of an incline to empty trucks thereby drawn back to the pit head. He and his friends played perilously around the stretch of Stephenson's 1822 line as it ran close to Silksworth.

4. *Hefænricæs Uard:* Heaven's guardian, from the first line of Caedmon's 'Song of Creation'.

6. Refers to the Easington Colliery Disaster of 1951 which features in a number of WM poems.

Bonny May morning: an explosion occurred at 4.35 a.m. on Tuesday 29th May.

Night Shift...First shift: 'by a tragic trick of fate this was the time that there were two shifts in the explosion district.' Northern Mine Research Society.

7. See note to 'Anna Navis', 'Fellside Bread', etc.

Song (A Wearside version) (174)

The original 'A U Hinny Burd' is a dandling song enumerating locations in Newcastle, Tyneside and south-east Northumberland. See *Northumbrian Minstrelsy*, ed. J. Collingwood Bruce and John Stokoe, Society of Antiquaries of Newcastle-upon-Tyne, p.120 (facsimile reprint Llanerch Publishers, 1998).

NOTES ON THE EDITORS

Peter Armstrong was born in 1957 at Blaydon-on-Tyne. His work has appeared in four main collections: *Risings* (Enitharmon Press, 1988), *The Red-Funnelled Boat* (Picador, 1998), *The Capital of Nowhere* (Picador, 2003) and *The Book of Ogham* (Shoestring Press, 2012), together with pamphlets *Madame Noire* (2008) and *Two Ceremonies at the Border* (2023), both from Shoestring. He worked full-time in the NHS as a mental health nurse and CBT specialist, contributing to research papers and text books. He was joint author, with Stephen Barton of CBT for *Depression: an Integrated Approach* (SAGE, 2019). He lives in Northumberland.

Jake Morris-Campbell was born in South Shields in 1988 and is the author of *Between the salt and the ash: a journey into the soul of Northumbria* (Manchester University Press, 2025). His poetry collection *Corrigenda for Costafine Town* (Blue Diode Press, 2021) was longlisted for the RSL Ondaatje Prize and Highly Commended in the 2022 Forward Prizes. A BBC/AHRC New Generation Thinker, Jake makes regular broadcast appearances on BBC radio. He often collaborates with creative practitioners and specialists on multidisciplinary art shows. Jake holds a PhD in Creative Writing from Newcastle University and is currently Teaching Fellow in Creative Writing at Liverpool John Moores University. He lives in Oswestry, Shropshire.

EU DECLARATION OF GPSR CONFORMITY

Books published by Bloodaxe Books are identified by the EAN/ISBN printed above our address on the copyright page and manufactured by the printer whose address is noted below. This declaration of conformity is issued under the sole responsibility of the publisher, the object of declaration being each individual book produced in conformity with the relevant EU harmonisation legislation with no known hazards or warnings, and is made on behalf of Bloodaxe Books Ltd on 22 May 2025 by Neil Astley, Managing Director, editor@bloodaxebooks.com.

No part of this book may be used or reproduced in any manner for the purpose of training artificial intelligence technologies or systems. The publisher expressly reserves *Marratide* from the text and data mining exception in accordance with European Parliament Directive (EU) 2019/790.